EDUCATING FOR DEMOCRACY
IN A CHANGING WORLD

Studies in the
Postmodern Theory of Education

Joe L. Kincheloe and Shirley R. Steinberg
General Editors

Vol. 271

PETER LANG
New York • Washington, D.C./Baltimore • Bern
Frankfurt am Main • Berlin • Brussels • Vienna • Oxford

EDUCATING FOR DEMOCRACY IN A CHANGING WORLD

Understanding Freedom in Contemporary America

EDITED BY
STEPHEN M. FAIN,
DAVID M. CALLEJO PÉREZ,
AND JUDITH J. SLATER

PETER LANG
New York • Washington, D.C./Baltimore • Bern
Frankfurt am Main • Berlin • Brussels • Vienna • Oxford

Library of Congress Cataloging-in-Publication Data
Educating for democracy in a changing world:
understanding freedom in contemporary America /
edited by Stephen M. Fain, David M. Callejo Pérez, Judith J. Slater.
p. cm. — (Counterpoints: studies in the postmodern theory of education; vol. 271)
Includes bibliographical references.
1. Education—Political aspects. 2. Critical pedagogy. 3. Democracy.
I. Fain, Stephen M. II. Callejo-Pérez, David M. III. Slater, Judith J.
IV. Series: Counterpoints (New York, N.Y.); v. 271.
LC71.E285   370.11'5—dc22   2006000717
ISBN 978-1-4331-0032-1 (hardcover)
ISBN 978-0-8204-7066-5 (paperback)
ISSN 1058-1634

Bibliographic information published by **Die Deutsche Bibliothek**.
Die Deutsche Bibliothek lists this publication in the "Deutsche
Nationalbibliografie"; detailed bibliographic data is available
on the Internet at http://dnb.ddb.de/.

Cover design by Sophie Boorsch Appel

© 2007 Peter Lang Publishing, Inc., New York
29 Broadway, 18th floor, New York, NY 10006
www.peterlang.com

All rights reserved.
Reprint or reproduction, even partially, in all forms such as microfilm,
xerography, microfiche, microcard, and offset strictly prohibited.

Acknowledgments

What began as a conversation about air travel in a hotel lobby became a two year endeavor to discover who we were as Americans in light of the events of September 11, 2001. In those two years, the authors have relied on the ideas, patience, and support of many people who believed that our work would find a voice and audience within the American public. As such we would like to thank Chris Myers, at Peter Lang, who believed that our book would provide a diverse voice to the questions of education and democracy; and the tireless series editors, Shirley Steinberg and Joe Kincheloe, who have always been supportive of our ideas and encouraged us to put them on paper. We also extend our gratitude to individuals who helped in the writing process: the authors for their words of wisdom, Set Sokol, Bernadette Shade, and the production department at Peter Lang; and to Sarah Selmer, who tirelessly worked on suggestions and ideas that helped to create a finished product.

Finally, this book would not be possible without the help of our families who were there with their love and support in a transcending way. Stephen Fain would like to thank his wife, Judi Fain. David M. Callejo would like to thank Emily McGinnis. Judith J. Slater would like to thank her husband, Martin Cole.

Contents

Introduction 1

Part I: Democracy, Freedom, and the Law

Stephen M. Fain
    Chapter 1: The Fundamentals of Freedom in the Modern World 7

David J. R. Frakt and Arthur N. Frakt
    Chapter 2: Roosevelt's Vision in Legal and Political Jeopardy 21

Robert Gutierrez
    Chapter 3: The Four Freedoms Viewed in Comparison to Traditional American Political Ideals 33

Part II: Intellectual Perspectives on the Four Freedoms

Lesley A. Northrup
    Chapter 4: The First Amendment, the Second Freedom, and the Third Millennium 43

Pablo Toral
    Chapter 5: Four Freedoms in a Global Context 57

Louis A. Pagliaro and Ann Marie Pagliaro
    Chapter 6: Freedom, Fear, and Terrorism in Democratic Societies 75

Steven Selden
> *Chapter 7: The Neoconservative Challenge to the Undergraduate Curriculum: The Case of the Intercollegiate Studies Institute and the American Council for Trustees and Alumni* 89

Part III: Finding Meaning in the Four Freedoms

David M. Callejo Pérez
> *Chapter 8: Studies: High School History as Racial Text*.....................103

Jennifer Deets
> *Chapter 9: Flags and Homeschooling: Symbols of Freedom and Democracy*..121

Donn C. Worgs and Leon D. Caldwell
> *Chapter 10: Democratizing Education: Lessons from the African American Experience* 131

Judith J. Slater
> *Chapter 11: Language of the Curriculum: Memes of Practice*..............143

Epilogue: The Evolution of the American Creed: Survival of the Fittest 155

List of Contributors 165

Introduction

The origin of these chapters is rooted in conversations that took place in the wake of the events of September 11, 2001, and the responses of the government and the people of the United States. The question that served as the catalyst for this project was never actually articulated but it was understood as we observed a nation gripped by fear act in a way that often challenged the very principles upon which the nation stood.

America is in the process of reshaping its priorities, and in doing so adjusting its focus to better fit contemporary needs is not new. The elasticity of the Constitution has allowed the nation to adjust to changing times while sustaining the core values of the nation and its people (Scalia, 1997). However, it is clear that there was a reexamination and a series of adjustments in the popular understanding of these core values in the aftermath of the Great Depression and World War II. Reflecting on these changes Derek Bok, President Emeritus of Harvard University, notes that "the question worth asking after a half-century of effort is how good a job the society has done of adapting its traditional style and institutions to a new and much more formidable set of challenges" (1996, pp. 12–13). Justice Anthony Scalia argues that when it comes to the Constitution and the laws great care must be exercised when interpreting and adjusting the law to fit the moment (1997). He closes his argument with the observation that "by trying to make the Constitution do everything that needs doing from age to age, we shall have caused it to do nothing at all" (p. 47). In the aftermath of the events of 9/11 America's core values are being tested. As the nation engages in a new war—a "war on terror"—we anticipate that there will be changes in American life.

The shock wave resulting from the events of 9/11 extended beyond the United States. Free governments around the world realized that terror knows no national boundaries. President Bush declared a war on terror by focusing his attention on Al-Qaeda and other Muslim groups associated with the Jihadist movements fundamentally opposed to the life styles in democratic countries. As the free world responds to the threat of terrorists, the freedoms enjoyed in democratic countries may be in jeopardy. When we are concerned and guided by fear masked as efforts to make things more secure, citizens in the free world may act in ways that undermine the fundamental principles of democracy.

In his 1941 State of the Union address President Franklin Delano Roosevelt defined the fundamentals of a free society in terms of four freedoms: freedom of speech, freedom of religion, freedom from fear, and freedom from want. He argued that these freedoms were entitlements of all people everywhere. As we pondered the state of affairs after September 11, 2001, we wondered what the state of democracy in this changing world was.

In his latest work, *Seeing*, José Saramago (2006) writes about the rules of law and how they are obeyed. Each person within a society accepts the rules of governance, the societal restrictions, in exchange for the privilege of living in a community with others. When that community no longer chooses, individually or collectively, to obey the rituals and habitual practices or conventions that surround those rules of law because they no longer are utile or effective, what is it that is enforced? Is it the rule of law or the conventions and practices that have grown up around it? This is not to say that the fundamental law (in this story the right to vote) is wrong, only that when it is practiced in an out of the ordinary way (in the novel by a majority casting blank votes in an election) the law (freedom to vote) has not been violated, but the practice of actually voting for one of the candidates has been turned upside down. Of course, since this is a novel, the blank votes cast by the majority of citizens are seen as subterfuge, heresy, an attack on the government, which is the enforcer of the rule of law as process. Have they really broken the law? They were promised the right, the freedom to vote. They did. What they are ultimately punished for is that they broke with convention; they did the extraordinary; and the government retaliates.

What has this to do with freedom? Well, are we (the brethren) less free when we exercise our right to abridge and modify the practices that have grown out of the law? Do we have to constantly look to the courts to modify those practices, to clarify what freedom means in light of contemporary society? Will the state somehow protect our freedoms from history as practices become far removed from the letter of the law? The compact the individual has with the state is one that is a social compact. We give up some of our rights as individuals to live with others in a community. This community may be large or small, yet we obey the rules in exchange for the government protection as it enforces the freedoms pledged to the populace. But, the interpretation of those practices is a trade-off, perhaps of one illness of practice for another. We are either blind to the fairness or unfairness of those practices, or we see all too well when they serve special interests, whether they be political, economic, or other, rather than serving the members of the community they were intended to protect.

Our rules of law change over time based on interpretation, and sadly by partisanship of government representation. The bases of our freedoms of course are the Constitution and Bill of Rights, but in fact the changing practices are pragmatic responses, designed to reflect the temper of the time that Oliver Wendell Holmes situated as appropriate interpretations, and this is both a blessing and a curse. When leadership is after its own ends, its own preservation, or special interests, and money and oil crowd out other possibilities or make choice not an option, it is necessary to find scapegoats and direct blame when things do not turn out well for the populace. We have much to place blame on: the left, the right, special interest groups, religious fanaticism, intrigue, subversion, and self-protection claims. Of course there is always FEMA.

To understand freedom in contemporary America, it is necessary to have watchdogs, people and groups that disclose when and where those freedoms are abridged. In an age when universities are also under attack under the guise of accountability and profits, who is left to shout out when and where freedom is being compromised? Who else speaks out for the people to say when the spirit of the freedoms that we expect to have has been transformed into practices and activities that continually limit the exercise thereof?

That is what the authors have done in this book. They have spoken out to show that to be truly free, we have to be aware and alert to instances of abridgement of our freedoms, whether it be freedom of speech, religion, from fear or want. Each author questions our freedoms and points out what is influencing the practices surrounding them. In doing this each has responded to the challenge posed by Richard Clark, former counterterrorism adviser to Presidents Reagan, George H. Bush, Clinton and George W. Bush ("... we need to encourage an active, critical and analytical debate in America about how that will best be done. And if there is another major terrorist attack in this country, we must not panic or stifle debate as we did for too long after 9/11") (Clark, 2004, p. xxi).

Each of these chapters questions the freedoms that the public believes and expects will be allotted to them as citizens. It is necessary to be vigilant to the limitations on alternatives and interpretation that can, in fact, under the guise of obeying, end up denying us our right to freedom of speech, religion, from want and fear. And, we have to be proactive as professionals, educators, as individuals, and as part of the larger community to make sure that those in power make sure that these freedoms are protected and promoted.

As the chapters in this book were compiled, we were keenly aware of the greatness of the American people and the importance of the United States as a living definition of a working democracy. In the United States the people are the government and this is consequential. We are better able to understand this when we consider the insights offered by Harvard professor John Rawls:

> A difference between liberal peoples and states is that just liberal peoples limit their basic interests as required by the reasonable. In contrast, the content of the interests of states does not allow them to be stable for the right reasons: that is, from firmly accepting and acting upon a just Law of Peoples. Liberal peoples do, however, have their fundamental interests as permitted by their conceptions of right and justice. They seek to protect their territory, to ensure the security and safety of their citizens, and to preserve their free political institutions and the liberties and free culture of their civil society. Beyond these interests a liberal people tries to assure reasonable justice for all its citizens and for all peoples; a liberal people can live with other people of like character in upholding justice and preserving peace. (Rawls, 1999. p. 29)

As this book goes to press, there is war in the Middle East and famine in Africa. There are victims of natural disasters in the United States who have been homeless for more than one year.

The questions raised by professor Rawls are not high on the national agenda. We are concerned that the American people may have lost sight of the centrality of the four freedoms so vital to FDR. We are concerned about our response to the important challenge of educating for democracy in a changing world.

References

Bok, D. (1996). *The state of the nation: Government and the quest for a better society*. Cambridge, MA: Harvard University Press.
Clark, R.A. (2004). *Against all enemies: Inside America's war on terror*. New York: Free Press.
Rawls, J. (1999). *The law of peoples*. Cambridge, MA: Harvard University Press.
Saramago, J. (2006). *Seeing*. Orlando: Harcourt.
Scalia, A. (1997). *A matter of interpretation: Federal courts and the law*. Princeton, NJ: Princeton University Press.

Part I

Democracy, Freedom, and the Law

Consider the terms Democracy, Freedom, and Law. To a student of American political culture these terms represent fundamental principles reflecting the nature, process and structure of the United States. The Constitution and the Bill of Rights provide a purposeful structure within which the concepts of democracy, freedom and the law become operationally defined. However, over time the precise meaning of these words may be lost while a spirit reflective of these terms remains. This spirit is often felt while the meaning is lost. This set of essays deals with the philosophical and international perspectives of Franklin Delano Roosevelt's Four Freedoms. Readers are advised to consider each piece in the collection as an opportunity to consider how freedom is being defined, appreciated and advanced in the early days of the twenty-first century.

Stephen M. Fain's chapter is foundational for this collection of essays. The piece traces the evolution of the principles and trends that have defined and explained dispositions of American leadership towards the establishment and subsequent management of the American democracy

David J. R. Frakt and Author N. Frakt present a careful analysis of how changes in politics and law have jeopardize the vision of America advanced by FDR in his Four Freedoms speech. The relationship between the people and the law as defined by the protections guaranteed by the Bill of Rights is examined and the findings of this analysis suggest that protections are in jeopardy. This chapter seriously considers the power of fear as a controlling force which can seriously undermine the cause of liberty in the name of security.

Robert Gutierrez offers readers an opportunity to consider the evolution of the role of government in the United States. This chapter explains how the US shifted from a minimalist democratic system of government where the individual's initiative was the centerpiece of the relationship between the government and the governed to a system more like European democracies where the government accepts certain responsibilities and obligations while limiting some basic freedoms. This shift in the American system is shown to be strongly connected to FRD's New Deal. The chapter challenges the reader to consider the implications of the current divide separating conservatives and progressives.

1
The Fundamentals of Freedom in the Modern World

STEPHEN M. FAIN

This, indeed, is the greatness of man: to be able to have faith. For faith is an act of freedom, of independence of our own limited faculties, whether of reason or sense-perception. It is an act of spiritual ecstasy, of rising above our own wisdom (Heschel, 1987, p. 118).

The Book of Exodus tells the story of the Israelites fleeing from Egyptian slavery across a divided Red Sea into freedom. Freedom, undefined and unexamined, stood as a catalytic concept that was more felt than understood by generations living under the rule of emperors and kings. For many the world was arranged into three classes: sovereigns, free men, and slaves. Sovereign rulers were in their places because of divine right and slaves were in theirs by capture or social stigma. Freemen were in neither class but often were enslaved by economic and other social conditions. It was generally here, in that class of individuals who where neither rulers nor slaves, that the faith of freedom was nurtured and the cost and nature of freedom considered.

Faith and Power: The American Experience in Context

The emergence of the United States as a powerful country in the late 1700s gave form to that faith called freedom, and that state of emancipation that resulted began to define freedom in the modern world. The intensity of the passion for emancipation expressed by Thomas Paine in *Common Sense* stands as a clear demonstration of this faith. Published in Philadelphia in January, six months prior to the birth of the new nation, his words were read by those who would eventually declare the unification of the colonies and their independence. *Common Sense* is a radical critique of the rule of kings and challenge to men who consider themselves free to act as free men, and understand the powers associated with these social and economic principles (Kramnick, 1986, pp. 105–112). Paine strongly encouraged the development of a Continental Charter; he stressed that "a charter is to be understood as a bond or solemn obligation, which the whole enters into, to support the right of every separate part, whether of religion, personal freedom, or property." Paine continues, "A firm bargain and a right reckoning makes long friends" (Kramnick, 1986, pp. v and 109). On April 19, 1775, the Minutemen clashed with the Redcoats at Lexington and Concord. On June 7, 1776, Richard Henry Lee of Virginia placed the following resolution before the Second Continental Congress, "that these United Colonies are, and of right ought to be, free and independent States" (Johnson, 1997, p. 154). On July 4, 1776, the Continental Congress adopted the *Declaration of Independence,* engaged the British in war, and began in promoting a great social experiment.

Thomas Paine, in his pamphlet called *The American Crisis,* observed:

> THESE are the times that try men's souls. The summer soldier and the sunshine patriot will, in this crisis, shrink from the service of their country; but he that stands by it now, deserves the love and thanks of man and woman. Tyranny, like hell, is not easily conquered; yet we have this consolation with us, that the harder the conflict, the more glorious the triumph. What we obtain too cheap, we esteem too lightly: it is dearness only that gives every thing its value. Heaven knows how to put a proper price upon its goods; and it would be strange indeed if so celestial an article as freedom should not be highly rated. Britain, with an army to enforce her tyranny, has declared that she has a right (not only to tax) but "to bind us in all cases whatsoever" and if being bound in that manner, is not slavery, then is there not such a thing as slavery upon earth. Even the expression is impious; for so unlimited a power can belong only to God. (1776, www.ushistory.org/paine/crisis/c-01.htm)

These words reflect the spirit of independence and the general understanding of freedom that those who signed the Declaration embraced and those who served in the Continental Army fought and, sometimes, died for. However, although the spirit was passionately held and the understanding widely agreed to, freedom for the American people was a carefully examined principle.

Establishing an Independent Nation

Although independence was declared on July 4, 1776, it was neither clearly defined nor fully achieved then. It was not until 1783 and when the Continental Congress approved the Treaty of Paris that peace was made with the United Kingdom. In 1781 the Articles of Confederation were adopted and a temporary national government was formed. It was not until 1787 that *The Constitution of the United States of America*, and the first ten amendments (The Bill of Rights), were ratified by nine of the thirteen states. And, it was not ratified by all of the states until 1791—fifteen years after independence was declared.

For more than a decade a collection of men from diverse backgrounds with differing dispositions struggled together in efforts to create an egalitarian government. These men knew one another and squared off in face-to-face political debate more often than not settled via compromise, they understood that the enterprise that brought them together was a great historical moment, and finally, they refused to allow the contentious issue of slavery to deter them from their mission. Scholars of this period often point to the relationship of John Adams and Thomas Jefferson as the classic example of the relationship that defined the interactions of those involved (see J. Ellis, 2000, pp. 16–18). The language traditionally used to classify and stratify the people such as *husbandman, yeoman,* and *esquire* were dropped and replaced by words such as *people* and *citizen*, and traditional national government was replaced by a Republican model. And the transformational social power of education would be accepted as a significant stepping stone on the path to individual social progress (see Johnson, 1977, pp. 178–180). These men were, in general, among the new aristocracy of the fledgling nation. Although many were rooted in humble beginnings, their labors bore fruit and when they gathered they were men of station and privilege. They knew and understood those they represented and they valued what they themselves had earned with respect to property and position. They were eager to capture and refine the positive spirit of liberation that permeated the land but they paid little attention to the social realities of poverty and oppression within their own world.

The collective vision of these men took final form in *The Constitution of the United States of America*. This document presented a foundation upon which the government of the nation would stand. And, although it began with the words "We the People," it set out a plan for the implementation of a republic—a nation governed by representative, not directly by the people. It is important to understand that all who signed the constitution did not fully embrace the document. Rather than being in complete agreement, the signers recognized the importance of the moment, the need to provide a contextual framework for the new government, and power of unity among the representatives. Imperfect as it may have been to individuals, it was a magnificent document when considered in terms of the collective. Benjamin Franklin expressed these sentiments as he spoke to the delegates:

> The opinions I have had of its errors I sacrifice to the public good. I have never whispered a syllable of them abroad. Within these walls they were born, and here they shall die. If every one of us, in returning to our constituents, were to report the objections he has had to it, and endeavor to gain partizans [sic] in support of them, we might prevent its being generally received, and thereby lose all the salutary effects and great advantages resulting naturally in our favor among foreign nations, as well as among ourselves, from our real or apparent unanimity. Much of the strength and efficiency of any government, in procuring and securing happiness to the people, depends on opinion, on the general opinion of the goodness of that government, as well as of the wisdom and integrity of its governors. I hope, therefore, for our own sakes, as a part of the people, and for the sake of our posterity, that we shall act heartily and unanimously in recommending this Constitution wherever our influence may extend, and turn our future thoughts and endeavors to the means of having it well administered. (www.lexrex.com/enlightened/writings/franklin_on_const.htm).

The farmers, craftsmen, and shopkeepers who participated in the American experiment in the earliest days were willing to engage natural, social, economic, and political frontiers and in doing so they began to define the character of the people and the nation. Hard work and perseverance paid off and there was a growing belief among the people that they, not just the social elite, were entitled to the finer things in life. There was an understanding that it was neither birth nor privilege but education that made the gentleman.

Finally, the new nation must be appreciated for what it was, a republic where the government was made up of elected representatives charged with the responsibility of serving the nation. The interrelationships between the legislative, judicial, and executive branches of this government were guided by a system of checks and balances and their direct relationship with the people was seen in either the electoral process or sustained political relationships. Franklin was astute when he observed that much of the "strength and efficiency of any government, in procuring and securing happiness to the people, depends on opinion, on the general opinion of the goodness of that government, as well as of the wisdom and integrity of its governors" (www.lexrex.com/enlightened/writings/franklin_on_const.htm). The people, through the electoral process, had the closest political relationship with the legislative and were most distant from the judiciary. The dynamics of this system may not have been fully understood and appreciated by most citizens but the results were. The quest for liberty and independence resulted in the creation of a republic that allowed and encouraged democracy to thrive.

Ensuring Individual Rights

The U.S. Constitution consists of seven articles, each of which addresses a vital structural element in the formation and maintenance of a national government. This new government effectively places a great deal of power in the hands of the governed; yet, it says virtually nothing about the rights of the people. This fact troubled Thomas Jefferson, who, in a letter to James Madison, explained that he did not like the

> omission of a bill of rights providing clearly and without the aid of sophisms for freedom of religion, freedom of the press, protection against standing armies, rejection against monopolies, the eternal and unremitting forces of the habeas corpus laws, and trial by jury in all matters of fact triable by the laws of the land . . . (as quoted in Hofstadter, 1958, pp. 113–114)

Madison and Jefferson argued over the creation of a bill or rights for some time. Madison was convinced that a bill of this kind would be of little value, while Jefferson believed that armed with such a bill the judiciary would be able to balance the legislature (the people) should conditions arise that could jeopardize the liberty of some because of the whim of a majority. Eventually, Madison was convinced that a bill of rights was warranted (see Levy, 1999, pp. 32–37).

By attaching the Bill of Rights (the first ten amendments) to the U.S. Constitution a connection was made that paralleled Jefferson's thinking regarding the principles of liberty with the life of the people. Of the ten amendments, the first eight detail the fundamental rights and freedoms of every American citizen. The Ninth Amendment prohibits the government from limiting freedoms and guarantees citizens' rights that are not listed in the U.S. Constitution. The Tenth Amendment limits the powers of the federal government to those who are granted that in the U.S. Constitution.

The Bill of Rights specifies the freedoms guaranteed to American citizens. However, there is little evidence to suggest that the citizens who enjoy these freedoms fully understood the specifics of each amendment. Rather, it appears that from the very beginning, Americans embraced freedom as a cultural reality, defined it by living it and feared losing it. An example supporting this view was the Alien and Sedition Acts passed by Congress in 1798 when there was fear of war with France. The Alien Enemy Act and the Alien Friends Act allowed the president to, respectively, imprison or deport citizens of an enemy nation and to deport those citizens of friendly nations if they thought them dangerous. The Sedition Act provided for fine or imprisonment of anyone who criticized the government or encouraged resistance to federal laws. Although resisted by members of the Republican Party, these laws remained on the books for about three years when they expired. Driven by fear it seems that defense of the practical often trumps the ideal for the common citizen.

Life, Liberty, and the Pursuit of Happiness

American citizens enjoy living in democracy even though there is very little evidence that most understand the significance of the founding documents and the insightful construct they have established. Alexis de Tocqueville visited America in the early 1830s and reported that the people exhibited a unique public spirit "nurtured by the laws ... (and) the exercise of civil rights ... (and) confounded with the personal interests of citizen" (1956, p. 103). He explained that the people of America enjoyed "general prosperity," which they attribute mainly to their own personal hard work. Ralph Waldo Emerson saw "Prosperity" "including the reliance on governments which protect it, is the want of self-reliance" (1987, p. 49). He went on to comment that "Men have looked away from themselves and at things so long, that they have come to esteem the religious, learned, and civil institutions as guards of property, and they deprecate assaults on these, because they feel them to be assaults on property" (1987, p. 49). Finally Emerson concludes his observation by explaining that men "measure their esteem of each other, by what each has, and not by what each is" (p. 49).

Americans have created a nation where economic prosperity and independence may well be the most powerful and popular defining characteristics of the nation. The preponderance of American historical fact, literature, and lore are filled with examples of persons arriving in this country with nothing and ending up having acquired wealth and social status. Americans, it would seem from the onset, have defined liberty and prosperity as the essential ingredients of happiness. There is substantial evidence supporting the fundamental importance of prosperity and independence to Americans. Additionally, there is a paucity of evidence that suggests that the American people never fully understood, embraced, or interacted with the general constructs that ensure the opportunities provided to them. The rights set down in the Bill of Rights appear to be known to Americans as the result of the process of acculturation.

For more than a century the United States moved upward from fledgling nation to one of great consequence. Under President Theodore Roosevelt the American navy was second in size only to the British and he used this force to uphold democratic republicanism and to expand the Monroe Doctrine. President Woodrow Wilson expanded on this international role as a mediator between China and Japan, intervening in Mexico and the Caribbean and eventually by joining Russia, France, and Britain and declaring war in 1914 against the Central Powers:

Germany, Austria-Hungary, and Turkey. During Wilson's administration liberties were curtailed with the passage of the Espionage Act (1917) and the Sedition Act (1918), and an anti-German propaganda campaign began. With the victory in 1918 in the Great War the United States established itself as a world power. However, at home, Wilson was not able to garner the necessary support for his plan for the League of Nations and fear gripped the nation as Communism was on the rise in Europe and the United States and there was concern for the economic future of the country.

Freedom in Modern Times

On January 6, 1941, Franklin D. Roosevelt, the thirty-second President of the United States, addressed the seventy-seventh Congress and described it as "unprecedented in the history of the union" (Roosevelt, 1941). He faced a Congress that had responded to his call for a declaration of War against the Axis Powers—Germany, Italy, and Japan. And, he faced a nation that had come to listen to him as he used the radio to effectively connect his policies with the people. On this day the president reached back into American history and grasped the founding documents and the principles therein as a foundation for his discourse on democracy. Knowing that terms such as liberty, freedom, and independence were personally appreciated and known as lived experiences but not as sophisticated philosophical principles, he crafted a message that could be clearly understood by the American people and all others who would listen. He committed himself and the nation to the defense at home and the advancement abroad of four fundamental freedoms:

> The first is freedom of speech and expression—everywhere in the world.
> The second is freedom of every person to worship God in his own way everywhere in the world.
> The third is freedom from want, that is, economic understandings that will secure to every nation a healthy peacetime life for its inhabitants—everywhere in the world.
> The fourth is freedom from fear, that is, a world-wide reduction of armaments to such a point and in such a thorough fashion that no nation will be in a position to commit an act of physical aggression against any neighbor—anywhere in the world.

Less than three weeks after delivering the Four Freedoms speech, President Roosevelt delivered his third inaugural address. This speech focused on the nation's faith in democracy and the democratic spirit of America and Americans. He noted that the United States provided vast opportunities to its citizens by protecting the freedoms guaranteed in the Bill of Rights, and he observed:

> That spirit—that faith—speaks to us in our daily lives in ways often unnoticed, because they seem so obvious. It speaks to us here in the Capital of the Nation. It speaks to us through the processes of governing in the sovereignties of 48 States. It speaks to us in our counties, in our cities, in our towns, and in our villages. It speaks to us from the other nations of the hemisphere, and from those across the seas the enslaved, as well as the free. Sometimes we fail to hear or heed these voices of freedom because to us the privilege of our freedom is such an old, old story.

The Four Freedoms provided a way for Americans to articulate the reason they supported the war. The Four Freedoms became a kind of social mantra uniting a nation and a cause. Norman Rockwell, the great American illustrator, presented each freedom in a folksy drawing filled with patriotic American nuances. And these drawings hung all across the nation as symbols of national unity and resolve in a time of war. In 1942 a booklet was published by the Office of War Information titled *The United Nations Fight for the Four Freedoms*, and in 1943 and 1946 U.S. postage stamps were issued commemorating the Four Freedoms.

Freedom and Fear in Post–World War II America

As World War II was ending, Roosevelt, Churchill, and Stalin met at Yalta to resolve their differences and establish an international institution dedicated to bringing all nations of the world together for peace and the advancement of programs grounded in the principles of social justice and human dignity. The first meeting of the United Nations took place in London in January 1946. In the same year Winston Churchill noted that "an iron curtain has descended across the Continent" dividing Europe with the Soviet Union controlling the nations behind it (Churchill [1946] as quoted in www.Fordham.edu/halsall/mod/churchill-iron.html, accessed Feb 5, 2007). Stalin did not disagree that Communism was spreading across the Continent. He argued that "the influence of the Communists grew because during the hard years of the mastery of fascism in Europe, Communists showed themselves to be reliable, daring, and self-sacrificing fighters against fascist regimes for the liberty of peoples." This was the beginning of the Cold War, a war that demonstrated the interconnectedness of nations and raised fears on both sides of the iron curtain.

In the United States there was a great fear of Soviet Communism. The collectivist principles of the movement were counter to the principles of independence, property rights, and the basic freedoms articulated in the Bill of Rights. Fearful of the Communist threat from within, in 1937 the House of Representatives established the Un-American Activities Committee (HUAC) for the purpose of investigating un-American and subversive activities. In 1947 the HUAC began an investigation into the Hollywood Motion Picture Industry. Initially the committee interviewed forty-one "friendly witnesses" who voluntarily came forward and accused others in the business of holding left wing views. The result of this effort was the creation of a "black list" that prevented scores of actors and writers from work.

Among the "friendly witnesses" who testified before HUAC was Ronald Reagan, president of the Screen Actors Guild and Walt Disney. Reagan had been a staunch Democrat and supporter of FDR. One of the interesting points in his testimony was his deep commitment to democracy and his strong opposition to the philosophy of the Communist Party. He closed his testimony with these words:

> I detest, I abhor their philosophy, but I detest more their tactics, which are fifth column, and are dishonest, but at the same time I never as a citizen want to see our country become urged, by either fear or resentment of this group, that we ever compromise with any of our democratic principles through that fear or resentment. I still think that democracy can do it. (As quoted in History Matters, n.d.)

Although already protected by the McCormack Act (1938) requiring the registration of foreign agents and the Hatch Act (1939), and the Smith Act (1940) that allowed for the prosecution of individuals who advocated the violent overthrow of the government, President Truman authorized inquiries into the associations and political beliefs of federal employees (Johnson, 1997, p. 833). In 1952 the Senate created the subcommittee on investigations that was chaired by Senator Joseph M. McCarthy. In an effort to protect the nation from Communist agents who had infiltrated the government and Communist sympathizers, especially those working in the media and teaching at colleges and universities, this committee actively sought to identify and purge Communists from all positions of influence within the country. When the Senator took on the army of the United States his reign of terror was shut down. He had taken the *Red Scare* to its end and his political witch-hunt was over. In November 1964 *Harper's* magazine described this phenomena as "the paranoid style in American politics."

Along with the concerns about Communist infiltration within the United States and the spread of Communism in Europe, there was also a fear of a Communist takeover of Asia. In 1954, at a press conference, President Eisenhower was asked to comment on the strategic importance of Indo-China.[1] He explained the strategic link connecting Indo-China, Burma, Thailand, the Peninsula, and Indonesia. He continued to discuss the strategic importance of Japan, Formosa, the Philippines, New Zealand, and Australia, and how they would have to be protected. His point was that if one fell, the others could fall in succession much like a line of standing dominoes. This *domino theory* was to later be the justification for U.S. involvement in the Vietnam War. The strong Soviet presence in Europe and the spreading of the Communist movement in Asia kept the heat on in the cold war.

Looking back to 1945, Studs Terkel, an insightful commentator on the American character, observed that in the shadows of the victory of World War II fear gripped the land as the memory of the bomb gripped the nation (2003, p. xxii). "The word *communist* had become the all-encompassing pejorative that was to include scores of thousands of liberal and left temperament. Fear had replaced hope as the temper of the land . . ." (2003, xxii).

The control exerted by the Communists subdued many, but there were those whose passion for freedom resulted in resistance. In 1956 the Hungarian people attempted to shed the yoke of communism in favor of a more democratic form of government only to be stopped in their tracks by the Soviet Union. In 1981 Lech Walesa led the workers at the Gdansk shipyards in a demonstration against the Communist regime that reignited a passion for freedom in the Polish people. Throughout the 1970s and into the 1980s, Vaclav Havel's plays focused on the oppression in Czechoslovakia and his imprisonment for subversion.

Moving to the Right

Prior to ascending to the presidency in 1981 Ronald Reagan served two terms as governor of California. It was in this capacity that he confronted Mario Savio, the force behind the Free Speech Movement that polarized the University of California at Berkeley and launched the anti-war student movement across the nation. In response to this movement Governor Reagan set his sights on winning the battle with the liberals. By the time he took office *liberal* was a discredited affiliation and the economic reforms and social policies associated with FDR's New Deal were being adjusted by both president and Congress. And, there was a general shift toward the *Right* among many whom once were strong supporters of the more liberal politics of the *Left*.

Nothing captures the power of this shift more eloquently than *The Contract With America*, a platform built on Ronald Reagan's 1985 State of the Union address, and released by the Republican Party just prior to the first mid-term election of the Clinton administration in 1994. Written mostly by Representative Dick Armey (Texas), and championed by Newt Gingrich (Georgia) and Tom DeLay (Texas), the contract resonated with a growing conservative electorate and the Republicans gained a majority in the 104th Congress for the first time in more than four decades. The contract promised tax reform, term limits, social security reform, tort reform, and welfare reform.

This new conservative congressional force was enough to pressure President Bill Clinton into signing the 1996 Welfare Reform Act. Also known as the 1996 Personal Responsibility and Work Opportunity Reconciliation Act, this legislation discouraged illegitimacy and unwed teen pregnancies by prohibiting welfare to mothers under eighteen years of age and significantly limiting *Aid to Families with Dependent Children* (AFDC) benefits for additional children of welfare mothers. It strategically addressed change in the nation's welfare system by requiring work in exchange for benefits and offering incentives to states that implemented workfare programs as replacements for welfare.

The new conservative power in Congress was driven by a vision of a system where the power of the citizen and local governments was increased while the distance between local authorities and the federal government was decreased. This vision was bolstered by a citizenry that embraced the principles of individualism, independence, and initiative and at the same time rejected welfare, unions, affirmative action, and the United Nations.

In his inaugural address (January 20, 2001) President George W. Bush proclaimed:

> America, at its best, is a place where personal responsibility is valued and expected.
>
> Encouraging responsibility is not a search for scapegoats; it is a call to conscience. And though it requires sacrifice, it brings a deeper fulfillment. We find the fullness of life not only in options, but in commitments. And we find that children and community are the commitments that set us free.
>
> Our public interest depends on private character, on civic duty and family bonds and basic fairness, on uncounted, unhonored acts of decency which give direction to our freedom.
>
> Sometimes in life we are called to do great things. But as a saint of our times has said, every day we are called to do small things with great love. The most important tasks of a democracy are done by everyone.
>
> I will live and lead by these principles: to advance my convictions with civility, to pursue the public interest with courage, to speak for greater justice and compassion, to call for responsibility and try to live it as well.
>
> In all these ways, I will bring the values of our history to the care of our times.
>
> What you do is as important as anything government does. I ask you to seek a common good beyond your comfort; to defend needed reforms against easy attacks; to serve your nation, beginning with your neighbor. I ask you to be citizens: citizens, not spectators; citizens, not subjects; responsible citizens, building communities of service and a nation of character.

Americans are generous and strong and decent, not because we believe in ourselves, but because we hold beliefs beyond ourselves. When this spirit of citizenship is missing, no government program can replace it. When this spirit is present, no wrong can stand against it.

Although these remarks may appear consistent with the spirit of the twentieth-century they represent a shift from a liberal to a conservative national disposition. This shift became more evident 8 months later when terrorists struck in New York and Washington, DC. (www.let.rug.nl/usa/P/gwb43/speeches/gwbush1.htm).

On September 11, 2001, President George W. Bush addressed the nation: " . . . Today, our fellow citizens, our way of life, our very freedom came under attack in a series of deliberate and deadly terrorist acts . . ." (www.whitehouse.gov/news/releases /2001/09/20010911–16.html). In the wake of the events of this day and these comments it is proper to ask what the state of our freedoms, our way of life are in this nation and around the world. With the cold war behind us and the economy robust, where were we as a nation, as a world, in terms of the four freedoms (freedom of speech and expression, freedom of religion, freedom from want, and freedom from fear) articulated by FDR on 9/11/2001 and where are we today?

In the following pages, the contributors to this volume hope to address some of the issues brought up in this book. The current volume is divided into three sections. In the first, we examine the problem as a legal matter relating to our civil liberties. The second section looks at the issue from a global perspective. And the last section examines the problems that belie education in the twenty-first century.

Notes

Throughout this chapter the term American will be used to denote citizens living in the United States of America. This has been done to allow for a smooth flow and is consistent with the language used in the literature cited.

1. President Harry S. Truman authorized economic and military aid to the French, who were engaged in a war for their colony. When the French were defeated in 1954 the country was divided into North and South Vietnam. The North was Communist and the South was not. President Eisenhower pledged U.S. support for the building of a free and democratic South Vietnam.

References

Bush, G. W. (2001). Statement by the President in His Address to the Nation. September 11. www.whitehouse.gov/news/releases /2001/09/print/20010911–16.html, accessed September 27, 2006.

Churchill, W. (1946). "The Sinews of Peace" as quoted in James, Robert Rhodes (1949). *Winston S. Churchill: His Complete Speeches 1897–1963*, New York: Chelsea House Publishers. Vol. VII, pp. 7285–7293.

Ellis, J. (2000). *Founding Brothers: The Revolutionary Generation*. New York: Vintage Books.

Emerson, R. (1987). *Ralph Waldo Emerson: Essays and Lectures*. New York: Library of America.

Heschel, A. J. (1987). *God in Search of Man*. Northvale. NJ: Jason Aronson Inc.

History Matters (n.d.). "We Must Keep the Labor Unions Clean": "Friendly" HUAC Witnesses Ronald Reagan and Walt Disney Blame Hollywood Labor Conflicts on Communist Infiltration. Retrieved on September 21, 2006, http://historymatters.gmu.edu/d/6458/

Hofstadter, R. (1958). *Great Issues in American History: A Documentary Record, 1864–1957*. (Vol. 2). NY: Vintage.

Jefferson, T. (1787) "Letter to James Madison on the Constitution" as quoted in Hofstadter, R. (1958). *Great Issues in American history: From the Revolution to the Civil War, 1765–1865*. New York: Vintage Books.

Johnson, P. (1997). *A History of the American People*. New York: Harper Perennial.

Kramnick, I. (Ed.). (1986) *Thomas Paine: Common Sense*. London: Penguin Books.

Levy, L. (1999). *Origins of the Bill of Rights*. New Haven, CT: Yale Nota Bene.

The Office of War Information (1942). *The United Nations Fight for the Four Freedoms*. Washington, DC: The Office of War Information.

Paine, T. (1776). *The American Crisis*. www.ushistory.org/paine/crisis/c-01.htm.

Roosevelt, F. D. (1941). *Third Inaugural*. http://www.bartleby.com/124/pres51.html, accessed September 13, 2006.

Terkel, S. (2003). *Hope Dies Last: Keeping the Faith in Difficult Times*. New York: The New Press.

de Tocqueville, A. (1956). *Democracy in America*. Trans. Richard. D. Heffner. New York: Mentor.

2
Roosevelt's Vision in Legal and Political Jeopardy

DAVID J. R. FRAKT AND ARTHUR N. FRAKT

In this chapter, we consider how the legal and political landscape has changed in ways that jeopardize Franklin Roosevelt's vision of a free and humane society as presented in his Four Freedoms speech.

At the turn of the millennium, the ideas and values expressed in the Four Freedoms speech were deeply ingrained in the American psyche. While there may have been some disagreement about the scope of freedom of speech, expression, the press and religion, there was strong national consensus that these freedoms were at the core of our national character. Similarly, the goals of freedom from want, or economic freedom, and freedom from fear, were widely agreed upon. At the time of this writing, in early summer 2006, after nearly five years of the "Global War on Terror," more than three years of the Iraq War and a concomitant attack on the domestic front against these cherished values, we are not so certain. Indeed, as a result of an increasingly conservative Supreme Court and an administration with highly different priorities than those of FDR, the Four Freedoms have never been in greater peril.

Prior to 9/11, we had been in a judicial era of unparalleled tolerance for minority, even radical opinions for over four decades. By contrast, in the era from World War I to the time of the Four Freedoms speech, governmental repression of those deemed dangerous and unpatriotic was sanctioned by both Congress and the courts. The principle support for freedom of expression was articulated in the dissenting opinions of Justices Holmes and Brandeis. While their views were ultimately vindicated during the Warren era, judicial tolerance for repression of speech continued through the post–World War II paranoia about internal Communist threats to our republic.

It is remarkable that through and after the Vietnam War, no significant legislative efforts were undertaken to limit political dissent, although a proposed constitutional amendment against flag burning as an unacceptable form of symbolic speech surfaces from time to time as an easy shorthand way for politicians to demonstrate patriotism. Within weeks of 9/11, hastily cobbled together legislation, misleadingly titled the USA PATRIOT Act, was enacted. Arguably, the PATRIOT Act does not directly limit freedom of speech, but it greatly increases the power of the government to engage in surveillance and monitoring of activities protected by the First Amendment. The PATRIOT Act's potential use as a tool to gain information on dissenters may well inhibit the full exercise of their rights. Also, the expanded definition of the phrase "providing material support" to terrorists has caused many to be fearful of exercising free expression by associating with political and charitable organizations that might advocate or support unpopular causes, particularly in the Middle East. Similar conclusions about the chilling effect on free speech may be drawn from the apparent widespread warrantless accumulation of information about the phone calls and other communication activities of Americans of all political persuasions.

Virtually every week in mid-2006 has brought news of the incursions of government agencies into areas of the private lives of Americans formerly believed to be inviolate, unless a neutral judicial officer had determined that there was good cause for the government's action and had issued a warrant carefully circumscribed as to time, place and manner. Whether it is financial transactions, private telephone calls, library use, travel, etc. the administration has demonstrated an arrogant disregard for either legislative or judicial oversight.

What is arguably of even greater concern than the government's ever-increasing encroachments on our privacy is the fact that the majority of Americans apparently support these efforts regardless of their dubious constitutionality, under the theory that those who have nothing to hide have no reason to be distressed about governmental snooping.

Another way that the current administration has sought to reduce political expression is by limiting the information available to the public and the press, so Americans can't make informed appraisals about what their government is doing. The federal courts have largely acquiesced in this.[1] The administration has reversed a long-standing trend towards government openness, embarked on a widespread campaign of reclassifying previously unclassified documents, and, under the rubric of national security, "executive privilege," or other pretexts, has consistently denied Freedom of Information Act and other legitimate requests for information.[2]

When a determined press corps has managed to uncover the administration's closely guarded secrets, such as CIA "ghost" prisons, illegal renditions, and secret NSA domestic wiretapping, the response of the executive branch has been to threaten prosecution of those who would dare to expose these abuses and to vilify the journalists as unpatriotic, even treasonous.

An article in the *New York Times* (June 4, 2006) reviewed the use of the "state secrets" privilege to eliminate lawsuits and concluded the Bush administration had used the privilege excessively. For example, whistleblowers who have been fired from government positions, individuals who had been seized and subject to "rendition" and secret imprisonment, and those who claimed that the government had discriminated against them in employment all had their cases dismissed after the administration claimed that consideration of the lawsuits would force the revelation of secrets important to national security. Thus far, in the nineteen cases during the Bush administration in which "state secrets" doctrine has been relied upon, the courts have acquiesced in every one without even holding confidential hearings into the merits of the claims.

Of course, the diminution of civil liberties during "wartime" is not a new phenomenon. Throughout history, when a threat to a nation's security is perceived by both the government and a majority of its citizens, judicial protection for individual and group rights has received short shrift. Nothing demonstrates this truth more clearly than the removal of American citizens of Japanese ancestry from their homes and businesses on the West Coast during World War Two. Families were forced into internment camps in barren and climatically hostile environments in violation of every significant right of citizenship, without any evidence that they posed a threat to our national security. The Supreme Court upheld these governmental actions in *Korematsu v. United States*, 323 U.S. 215 (1944), and *Hirabayashi v. United States*, 320 U.S. 81 (1943). At the time of these infamous cases, Earl Warren, the Chief Justice who today is rightly revered as a great protector of civil liberties, was the Attorney General and then Governor of California and a vigorous proponent of the internments. Franklin Roosevelt was President and the Court's opinions were written by Chief Justice Harlan Fiske Stone (Hirabayashi) and Hugo Black (Korematsu). That these two leaders should have acquiesced in the Supreme Court's movement to afford greater federal protection to civil liberties in this most notorious suppression of rights speaks volumes about the pressure to compromise civil liberties in wartime. But, importantly, the United States later admitted that the internment of Japanese-American civilians had been wrong and offered apologies and compensation for its misdeeds.

What is different about the "war on terror" from previous armed conflicts is that excessive government limitations on civil liberties usually ended or were significantly ameliorated when the conflict ended; in contrast, this war, because of its vague and general nature, threatens to affect our national policy far into the future. Another troubling development has been the Bush administration's insistence on an expansive understanding of its authority, coupled with a concomitant decrease in congressional oversight and control. Thus, we now face the prospect of ever-greater limits on individual rights with no clear end in sight.

It is not only our freedom of expression that is currently threatened, but also the notion of freedom from want, which FDR defined as "economic understandings which will secure to every nation a healthy peace time life for its inhabitants—everywhere in the world." Clearly this vision of equality of economic opportunity and global prosperity has not been realized in large sections of our planet; Hurricane Katrina helped to expose the extent to which economic opportunities have failed to reach urban African-Americans. Less dramatically, economic justice for all Americans is being threatened by a subtle but clear reinterpretation of certain constitutional principles.

Beginning in the late 1930s through the 1960s, the Supreme Court followed a consistently developing course in constitutional interpretation. The Court's majority used a combination of an expansive reading of the Commerce Clause and the Equal Protection and Due Process clauses to expand the constitutional reach of the Court to both validate federal civil rights and social justice legislation and to overturn state and local laws and activities which interfered with personal rights and liberties.

In a brief chapter, it is impossible to fully explicate the revolutionary changes in constitutional doctrine that took place in the forty-year period that ended with the ascendance of Chief Justice Warren Burger and the corresponding increase in the number of conservative "strict constructionist" Justices. A summary of these developments must suffice.

The Bill of Rights was directed against excesses of the federal government and not of those of the states or local authorities. In fact, the First Amendment that contains the critical clauses concerning freedoms of speech, assembly, the press, and religion, specifically applies only to Congress and not to state legislatures. Gradually, the mid-twentieth century Supreme Court adopted a theory of "incorporation" using the Due Process and Equal Protection clauses of the Fourteenth Amendment. The incorporation theory holds that the freedoms of the First Amendment and some other key provisions of the Bill of Rights are so fundamental to a free society that they apply to actions by the states and their political subdivisions to the same extent that they limit the federal government.

A view that the rights expressed in the First Amendment are not static was also critical to the development of protection for other civil liberties. Under this view, when the First Amendment is read in context with the Ninth Amendment (which states that "the enumeration of rights shall not be construed to deny or disparage others retained by the people") and the Due Process clauses of the Fifth and Fourteenth Amendments, the Court could enunciate a more expansive theory of personal liberty. This is how the right of privacy, which is not mentioned in the original Bill of Rights, became a protected civil liberty. The right of privacy has been central to our contemporary approach to reproductive rights.[3] In addition to the "new" right of privacy, rights explicitly found in the Fourth, Fifth and Sixth Amendments were all given expansive interpretation during this period of judicial liberalism. These include the right to counsel, and the rights to be free from unreasonable searches and seizures and compelled self-incrimination.

At the same time the Court was expanding the scope of free expression, it enunciated a doctrine of equality for racial minorities and upheld federal legislation that eliminated discriminatory practices in the Southern and border states. It did this partially through the reinvigoration of the post–Civil War amendments. The Thirteenth Amendment barred slavery. The Fifteenth Amendment protected the right to vote. Most significantly, the Fourteenth Amendment addressed several critical subjects. It declared citizenship for all those "born or naturalized in the United States." This applied not only federally, but also in the "State wherein they reside." The Fourteenth applied "due process" and "equal protection" directly against state action and it forbade the states to "abridge the privileges and immunities of citizens." All of these amendments had been construed very narrowly or ignored through the first half of the twentieth century. In the Warren era, the Court took a broad view of what constituted "state action" to which these amendments applied. With regard to discrimination in businesses such as restaurants, hotels, and stores, the Court expansively interpreted the Commerce Clause that gave Congress the power to "regulate commerce with foreign nations and among the several states." Congressional authority was enhanced by a clause which afforded Congress the authority to enact laws "necessary and proper" to carry out its constitutional mandates.[4]

Over the past two decades, an increasingly conservative Supreme Court, under the leadership of the late Chief Justice William Rehnquist (recently replaced by Chief Justice John Roberts), has placed this liberal Warren era jurisprudence in peril. Recent decisions have called into question the willingness of the federal government and the Supreme Court to ensure that big business, narrow parochial interests, and state and local powers with little concern for individual and minority rights do not regain the dominant power they held prior to 1940. While the Court's language is often arcane and murky, its intent to limit federal power is clear. For example, before Congress may act to address state actions that violate individual rights, "there must be congruence and proportionality between the injury to be prevented or remedied and the means adopted to that end" *City of Boerne v. Mores*, 521 U.S. 507 (1997).

This language has the effect of creating a balancing test which conservative federal courts may utilize to deny congressional authority to legislate where rights are threatened except in those circumstances where the courts will determine that there is no other conceivable remedy. Similarly, the power of Congress to enforce the provisions of the Fourteenth Amendment is restricted to those instances in which there is a history of "widespread and persistent deprivation of constitutional rights." In the *Boerne* case, the Supreme Court held unconstitutional the Religious Freedom Restoration Act (1993) that protected churches and religious organizations from the excessive burdens of state and local laws such as zoning regulations even if they appeared neutral on the surface. The Court seemingly elevated the value of local control above the value of religious freedom.

Using similar criteria, the Supreme Court has held that United States patent laws could not be enforced against the states (*Florida Prepaid Postsecondary Education Expense Board v. College Savings Bank*, 527 U.S. 627 [1999]). In the following year, the Age Discrimination in Employment Act was held unenforceable against the states (*Kimel v. Florida Board of Regents*, 528 U.S. 62 [2000]).

In these and other cases that curtailed the scope of the Commerce Clause and narrowed the reach of the Fourteenth Amendment, the Court majority included the conservative justices: Rehnquist, Scalia, Thomas, Kennedy and O'Connor. Justice O'Connor, considered the most moderate of the conservative justices, has now been replaced by the staunchly conservative Samuel Alito. In the limited number of decisions which have been issued since Justice Alito ascended to the bench, he has lined up squarely with the most conservative of the justices, Scalia and Thomas. Chief Justice Roberts has not deviated from the conservative positions of his predecessor. The dissenters, who applied the standards developed by the Warren Court, were Justices Stevens, Souter, Breyer and Ginsburg. Justice Kennedy, who may now be considered the "swing" vote, has generally been more conservative in his views than his retired colleague, Justice O'Connor.

A good example of the significant change in the Supreme Court's balance is found in a recent decision in which the five member conservative majority held that evidence found during a search would not be excluded from evidence in a subsequent criminal trial for failure of the police to knock and announce their presence (*Hudson v. Michigan*, 547 U.S. ___ [2006]). The Court had previously held that the so-called "knock and announce" rule was a requirement of a reasonable search under the Fourth Amendment (*Wilson v. Arkansas*, 514 U.S. 927 [1995]), and had repeatedly held that when police searches are unreasonable, the "fruits" of those searches must be excluded.[5] The Court had quite reasonably concluded in many prior cases that the only meaningful deterrent for police abuses of citizens' constitutional rights was the threat of having the evidence suppressed. The rationale for this reversal of many decades of interpretation of the Fourth Amendment exclusionary rule is that the "social costs" of exclusion (i.e., criminals being set free) outweighed the deterrent value of exclusion (or perhaps more accurately, outweighed the importance of the right itself). Justice Scalia also suggested that a better trained and more professional police force could be relied upon not to abuse their power and that the option of a civil suit against the police for abuses of their authority would be an adequate remedy available to those victimized by the police actions, a view that Justice Breyer characterized as a "support free assumption." In fact, the Supreme Court has long recognized that civil remedies for those whose rights are violated by law enforcement officials are wholly inadequate. Justice Breyer commented:

> As Justice Stewart, the author of a number of significant Fourth Amendment opinions, explained, the deterrent effect of damage actions "can hardly be said to be great," as such actions are "expensive, time-consuming, not readily available, and rarely successful." 547 U.S. ___.

That Justice Scalia should embrace civil damage suits as the sole remedy for violations of the Fourth Amendment devalues this critically important protection against police abuses.

Another ominous decision from the same five conservative members of the Supreme Court held that an assistant prosecutor in California who reported to his superiors that a search warrant had been improperly obtained did not have any First Amendment protection against retaliation by those superiors because his statements were made "pursuant to . . . official duties" and not as a citizen (*Garcetti v. Ceballos*, 126 S. Ct. 1951 [2006]). This truly absurd and unworkable distinction was dismantled in two well-reasoned dissents by Justice Souter (joined by Justices Stevens and Ginsburg) and Justice Breyer.

It should also be clear that the characterization of the more liberal justices as "activist" will not bear scrutiny. Judges have the power to determine controversies which come before them. The nature of decision-making is in itself an "activist" exercise. When conservative justices impose their own political and philosophical predilections and presume facts not in evidence, they are every bit as "activist" as their more liberal colleagues. A perfect example of this was the case of *Bush v. Gore* (531 U.S. 98 [2000]), which arguably determined the result of the 2000 presidential election. In that decision, the conservative majority of the Court (Justices Rehnquist, Scalia, Thomas, O'Connor, and Kennedy) reached out to utilize equal protection principles to overcome state court decisions in a manner which they had consistently rejected in civil liberties cases.

The principal philosophical basis for the conservative approach to constitutional jurisprudence has been what Justice Scalia calls an "originalist" approach to the

Constitution. As described in a recent speech that the Justice gave to a selected audience in Wyoming, this approach is, simply stated, a literal reading of the Bill of Rights. If a right is not defined specifically in the original language, it does not exist, and the use of Equal Protection and Due Process to consider the rights set forth expansively is forbidden. Justice Scalia takes the position that any expansion of civil liberties requires an amendment to the Constitution. Not only would this require an extremely difficult and time-consuming procedure, with the consent of two-thirds of each house of Congress and three-fourths of the states, but it is a totally unrealistic approach to important civil liberties issues which would be extremely difficult to set forth in the kind of factual "originalist" language that Justice Scalia favors. For example: how would a right of personal privacy be enshrined in a constitutional amendment? "Congress shall make no law limiting an individual's right to privacy?" By its very nature, "privacy" like "due process" and "equal protection," not to mention the liberties enshrined in the Bill of Rights, requires judicial interpretation for it to be an effective protection. Every personal liberty must, at some point, give way to other societal imperatives. Free speech cannot include "the right to falsely shout 'fire' in a crowded theater"; freedom of the press cannot include the right to publish the movement of troopships in wartime; freedom of religion cannot permit human sacrifice; and the right of privacy cannot extend to protect criminal conspiracies. To argue that the Constitution simply protects absolutely what is set forth in the Bill of Rights and nothing more is a position which no Justice has ever adhered to in his or her consideration of real cases.

Why does this matter? Without the expansive view of constitutional protections promulgated by a liberal Supreme Court, both civil rights and economic fairness are in danger of being severely curtailed. Reproductive freedom is based upon a broad reading of the "penumbra" of the Bill of Rights, including the First Amendment liberties and the Ninth Amendment that preserves unspecified rights to the people. Since the right of privacy is not mentioned in the Constitution, a strict constructionist Court could easily rule that legislatures could limit birth control and abortion in any way they chose. South Dakota has recently decided to test the new Court by criminalizing all abortions. Until recently it seemed unlikely that the Supreme Court would return to the pre-1936 era when the so-called "right of contract" was held to prevail over federal efforts to promote safe workplaces and to regulate the abuse of women and children by unscrupulous employers. Still, the danger that these protections will be left to the unpredictable and inconsistent actions of the individual states is very real. With the new membership of the Court, the rights of the accused, protection of minorities, and limits on state and federal interference with essential liberties may be in jeopardy; if one or two more Justices who adhere to the judicial philosophy of Justices Scalia, Thomas and Alito join the Court, the loss of cherished freedoms is a virtual certainty.

The national move to the right in our political ideology also threatens to erase gains we have made in the area of freedom from want. Since Theodore Roosevelt left office in 1909, a majority of the Republican Party has opposed virtually every legislative effort to improve the quality of life for the poor, for minorities, for women and children. With comfortable majorities in both houses of Congress and a decidedly pro-business, anti-tax, administration in the White House, many conservatives are making determined efforts to dismantle or destroy Social Security, Medicare and Medicaid through a combination of legislative, administrative and fiscal activities. Public education, environmental protection and essential scientific research are also under threat of destructive modification. Public acquiescence in these efforts is encouraged by an endless marketing and public relations campaign of Orwellian proportions, with heavy use of misleading labels and slogans such as "No Child Left Behind," the "Healthy Forests Initiative," "Saving Social Security Through Private Investment," and the "Death Tax." Perhaps most misleading is the USA PATRIOT Act (which is actually an acronym for "Uniting and Strengthening America by Providing Appropriate Tools Required to Intercept and Obstruct Terrorism"), which implies by its title that it is unpatriotic to oppose the widespread infringement of civil liberties which it authorizes. Unfortunately, it may be that in this era of short attention spans and limited critical analysis, effective labeling and simple lies will triumph over complex truths.

In our view, a good part of the reason for this political sea-change may be determined by an analysis of the events and issues that framed the Four Freedoms speech and the changed circumstances which confront contemporary society as it grapples with the application of Franklin Roosevelt's principles.

First, consider the legislative context. In 1941 the United States was still a substantially rural nation of 140 million. State legislatures were excessively dominated by representatives from under-populated counties to the disadvantage of urban dwellers. For example, while New Jersey's lower house membership was determined by population, its upper house had one senator from each of the state's counties. Thus, counties like Cape May and Sussex with just a few thousand residents had the same senatorial representation as Essex and Hudson with several hundred thousand citizens. This pattern was repeated in almost all of the states. By nature, these legislatures were extremely conservative and their activities could be dominated by a handful of powerful interests: agriculture, mining, manufacturing, and so on. It was not until 1962 that the Supreme Court, in a series of cases beginning with *Baker v. Carr*, 369 U.S. 186 (1962), ruled that both state legislatures and the federal House of Representatives had to be apportioned on the basis of population and that districts had to be rationally drawn to represent compact and contiguous geographic areas. As Chief Justice Warren put it, "Legislators represent people, not trees or acres. Legislators are elected by voters, not farms or cities or economic interests" (*Reynolds v. Sims*, 377 U.S. 533 [1964]). Over the next several years, redistricting gave much greater power to urban voters. Civil rights legislation increased the influence of African American voters and minority legislators. The result was a revolutionary growth in state and federal social and economic legislation including public accommodations laws, Medicare, Medicaid, the Environmental Protection Act, and so on. Thus many of the goals espoused in the Four Freedoms speech were enacted into law. Recently, these dynamic legislative developments have come to a grinding halt. How has this come about?

In the past few years, the sophisticated use of computer models and polling data along with increased judicial tolerance for legislative districts that more closely resemble Rorschach inkblots than rectangles have permitted incumbent legislative majorities of both parties to create non-competitive state and federal legislative districts. Ominously, the Supreme Court recently permitted the extreme mid-decade gerrymandering of the Texas congressional districts to stand, with Chief Justice Roberts and Justice Alito joining Justices Scalia, Thomas and Kennedy (*League of United Latin American Citizens v. Perry*, 548 U.S. ___ [2006]). The Court did declare that the Texas legislature's elimination of a majority Latino district violated the Voting Rights Act. (Id.) (Justice Kennedy switched sides in this part of the decision.) It is now clear that if the four most conservative justices are joined by one other in the same political mold, the democratization of Congress and state legislatures will have come to an end. Isolating voters by party or by race, dividing majority voting groups among multiple districts where they become a minority, or grouping most dissident voters in a single district so the dominant party can control several districts have all become common features of the political landscape. As a result, only a small percentage of state and federal legislative contests are competitive. For example, a recent *Cook Political Report* analysis of the upcoming 2006 congressional election places an astoundingly low 12 of 435 races in the truly competitive "toss-up" category, with another 34 races in the moderately competitive "lean" category.[6] In total, only about 11% of the races are competitive. Safely ensconced in a protected voting environment, legislators can ignore troubling issues and voters with whom they do not agree. They may sell their votes to their major contributors or simply adhere to the party line.

Serious consideration of differing viewpoints has become rare on both domestic and foreign policy issues. Internationally, our conduct has increased tension and fear. The invasion and occupation of Iraq and the notorious problems at Abu Ghraib and Guantanamo have increased the influence of radical Islamists in the Middle East. Our dismissive attitude toward international treaties, such as the Geneva Convention and Kyoto Protocol on global warming, and our refusal to support the International Criminal Court have resulted in America being perceived as an arrogant bully in much of Europe and the Western world.

Fortunately, the Supreme Court has drawn the line at the most egregious of the administration's legal positions: that the Guantanamo detainees could be held indefinitely, without charge, without access to attorneys, and could not challenge the legality of their detention in U.S. courts (*Rasul v. Bush*, 542 U.S. 466 [2004]). But even this seemingly unassailable decision was not unanimous. Frighteningly, three of the Justices (Scalia, Thomas, and Rehnquist) dissented, agreeing with the administration's view that the detainees' petitions for *habeas corpus* were unreviewable. In a related case, *Hamdan v. Rumsfeld*, 548 U.S. ___ (2006), the majority of the Court held that the Military Commission set up by President Bush to try Guantanamo detainees was invalid. The Court found the Commission exceeded presidential authority in the absence of specific congressional authorization. The Court also held that the Commission's procedures were so lacking in due process that they violated U.S. and international law, specifically the Uniform Code of Military Justice and the Geneva Convention. Again, three Justices (Scalia, Thomas and Alito) dissented, offering the view that the Court had no jurisdiction to hear the case, and even if it did, the Commission was perfectly valid. Because the Court was reviewing a decision made by Chief Justice Roberts when he was on the Court of Appeals, he had to recuse himself, but it is clear that he would have cast his vote with the dissenters. Again, one more politically conservative appointment to the Court could have yielded a very different result.

The values and goals espoused by President Roosevelt in his Four Freedoms speech, which not so long ago seemed both widely shared and attainable, have yielded in this administration to greed, aggression, intolerance, and secrecy. By straying from these principles, America has lost its place as the moral leader of the world. Fanatically inspired terrorism is a threat to the civilized world. But, ironically, the greatest threat to the Four Freedoms today arises not from without, but from within. The current administration's policies encourage fear, discourage a free exchange of ideas, and create want by limiting the reach of social legislation. Meanwhile, an increasingly reactionary Court has abandoned its role as a prime protector of individual and minority rights.

Were President Roosevelt alive today, he would surely be dismayed that his optimistic vision of a national government that encourages and supports all of our people as they seek healthier and more prosperous lives in a world of peace has been replaced with a vision that disdains the role of government as a vehicle for social justice.

Notes

1. See, e.g., *Cheney v. United States District Court*, 542 U.S. 367 [2004].

2. See, generally, the Project on Government Secrecy of the Federation of American Scientists http://www.fas.org/sgp/bush/index.html; See also, http://www.ombwatch.org/article/articleview/1145/1/18.
3. See *Griswold v. Connecticut*, 381 U.S. 479 [1965], (upholding the right of unmarried individuals to have access to contraceptives); see also *Roe v. Wade*, 410 U.S. 113 [1973], (a woman's right to privacy overcomes the state's interest in protecting a fetus, at least prior to viability).
4. See, for example, *Heart of Atlanta Motel*, 379 U.S. 241 [1964].
5. See *Mapp v. Ohio*, 367 U.S. 643 (1961); See also, the Appendix to Justice Breyer's dissent in *Hudson*, which lists 41 cases in which the Supreme Court has suppressed evidence or remanded to a lower court for a suppression determination for Fourth Amendment violations, 547 U.S. ___.
6. (http://www.cookpolitical.com, Retrieved on October 2, 2006).

3

The Four Freedoms Viewed in Comparison to Traditional American Political Ideals

ROBERT GUTIERREZ

In our collective memory, the Four Freedoms issued by the Roosevelt administration in the early 1940s have a dubious place of prominence. Morgan's (1985) biography of Franklin D. Roosevelt does not even refer to them. It probably would have an even more diminished place if it were not for Norman Rockwell's vision of each freedom as captured in his series of paintings. Garraty's (1979) history of America does make mention them in passing as part of Roosevelt's propaganda initiative to sell his proposed Lend-Lease program to save Great Britain from Hitler's aggression. One can safely believe that by the early 1940s, the administration was acutely aware of Hitler's menace not only to U.S. interests in Europe and North Africa, but also of his antithesis toward cherished American political values.

By the early 1940s, the nature of the totalitarian German regime was clear, although the depth of its inhumanity was yet to be made known. Those foreign realities, though, are only part of the context in which the Four Freedoms were issued. There was also a domestic context that, whether consciously thought of or not, still makes the content of the Four Freedoms not only meaningful, but also reflecting a departure from traditional American political values. The resulting tension is still with us today and serves as the basic question around which our national political discourse revolves.

The relevant domestic realities, of course, include the devastating economic depression that the nation was working itself out of with the advent of the war demand emanating from Europe. To meet the depression, the federal government under FDR embarked on a massive program, popularly known as the New Deal, that aimed at instituting, to varying degrees of longevity, governmental initiatives that provided relief, recovery, or reform. The result was a significant departure in American expectations for the role of government. Given the popularity of FDR, one is tempted to believe that the departure was readily accepted by the population of the United States. That is, the nation was not only practically disposed to the change, but culturally, the changes were insignificant or that if significant, the Great Depression had shifted the political culture enough to make the New Deal amenable to a new political ethos.

The truth could be that only the seriousness of the Great Depression made the basic principles of the New Deal temporarily appealing and that once the memory of those hard times diminished, the basic political beliefs challenged by the assumptions of the New Deal reestablished themselves among the American population. In this context, then, the Four Freedoms serve as a reflection of a time when basic questions concerning our political beliefs were being tested. One can view the four statements as a transition. They contained traditional claims of liberty, long held in the United States, and new claims that could aid in not only addressing the menace of totalitarian regimes, but also in justifying the efforts of the New Deal. The Four Freedoms provided language toward institutionalizing those reforms. That new language was suitable not only for the realities found within the United States, but also was applicable to the realities facing all industrial countries. The totalitarian regimes of Italy, Germany, and the Soviet Union had all put into effect automatic ideologies to meet the dislocations caused by adapting to industrial economies (Elazar, 1992). They were automatic in the sense that implementation of those ideologies promised utopian type results. Counting on individuals with their initiative and self-industry, on the other hand, was seen as inefficient and impractical and would lead toward selfish aims contrary to national interests or human justice.

Two Views of Rights

In order to analyze these tacit dynamics, Isaiah Berlin's (1984) "Two Concepts of Liberty" would be helpful. Berlin makes a distinction between positive and negative freedoms or rights. Positive rights are those rights that individuals have as human beings and it is government's responsibility to provide whatever program or policy to ensure their fulfillment. For example, a person is guaranteed health care services because he/she has a positive right to good health. In contrast, a negative right is a guarantee that a right an individual has will not be taken away by government action. For example, U.S. tradition is that the government cannot pass a law that prohibits one from participating in an assemblage. These need not be inalienable rights, rights that cannot be limited no matter what the situation (none of the rights listed in the Bill of Rights are inalienable), but the government needs to show a reasonable state interest before it limits or deprives an individual of such a right. Of course, all of these proscriptions are stated under the assumption of legality, that is, a government acting under a legal structure.

When one applies this distinction to the Four Freedoms, two of the freedoms are of a negative sort (freedom of religion and freedom of speech) and two are positive (freedom from want and freedom from fear). While a review of the Preamble of the U.S. Constitution identifies, in its broadest sense, a list of positive guarantees (e.g., to ensure domestic tranquility), these claims are too general for the point being made here. They can be seen as a list of reasons for the existence of government in the first place. More specific positive rights, such as good health and the like, are absent in our national constitution or our state constitutions (a significant exception is the right to an education found in our state constitutions). At the national level, our tradition, a federal tradition, has been to rely heavily on individual initiative or local political arrangements to meet concerns such as those over fear and want, be they economic, social, or political. This bias is reflected in the fact that, unlike in most European nations (influenced by a centralized political culture) and other democracies around the world, the U.S. system has a noncentralized system. Centralized systems are in a political position to address such concerns for a whole nation.

In line with this distinction, European nations can be characterized as Jacobin democracies and the United States has a federal democracy. The New Deal upset this constitutional bias in the United States. All of a sudden, the federal government, in an unusually centralized manner by U.S. standards, was attempting to institute a series of programs that in effect made the claim that American citizens were entitled to a series of positive rights. Of note is the fact that these changes were not made by changes to the constitution, but through statutory (legislative) laws. Included in these rights are welfare, especially for needy children, a job (if only temporary), or economic viability in old age. People's savings were now protected in banks and if they lost their jobs, they were entitled to monetary payments in order to survive the hard time until a new job was acquired. Law now defined the length of their workweek and, in like manner, the pay for overtime was determined. Traditionally, all of these concerns were expected to be defined by individuals as they negotiated the terms of contractual relations to which they agreed. State governments begrudgingly regulated the terms of such arrangements. The new view introduced by New Deal legislation of providing such rights is, even today, highly problematic to our national notions of liberty. European and other democratic nations, such as South Africa, not only protect positive rights as those contained in the New Deal by law but, unlike the United States, they enshrine them in their constitutions. This is due, as identified earlier, to their Jacobinist tradition.

Jacobism originated with the French Revolution. The Jacobins were the political group that captured power in France after the overthrow of Louis XVI. Their beliefs of governance relied on a strong state role in the affairs of people's lives. Central governmental power was already a feature of European politics. This was established with the Treaty of Westphalia that predated the French Revolution. What the Jacobists helped accomplish was institutionalizing such a view of government in Europe. To govern under such a view was to capture the state. Jacobist regimes hold to this principle by providing lengthy constitutions that spell out and define the legal and legitimate process by which a group takes over the state (Elazar, 1992).

Centralization is enhanced under this tradition by the process of attaining and instituting governmental programs. Jacobist systems deemphasize localism and diversity and instead seek unanimity. This unanimity is sought by attempting to bring the people together under a program of government policy collectively seen as the general will. In turn, the general will is formulated by a party or cadre that believes its members have a special insight or sensitivity to the national needs, to the concerns of its citizens. In a Jacobist democracy, winning an election entitles that party to institute its program, basically uncontested, and implement the constitutional and/or statutory provisions they deemed necessary. The "platform" that such parties run on take a more ideological aura, often stated in revolutionary language. Diversity is seen as an anathema to what it means to be a French person or whatever the nationality in question. Unanimity, with a relatively narrow definition of what is considered acceptable variance, is highly honored (Elazar, 1992).

This centralist view is contrary to U.S. tradition. The federalist tradition of this nation looks to divide power, making legislation difficult to enact, and institutionalizing processes that not only accept diversity, but in many ways encourage it. American high school government courses teach the "principles of the U.S. Constitution" and these summarize how our constitutional view differs from the Jacobist view. The principles are consent of the governed, separation of powers, checks and balances, federalism, limited government, and individual rights.

Elazar (1992) argues that American federalist democracy is supported by three dimensions. In order of popular preference, they are a civil society dimension, a public dimension, and a governmental dimension. In brief, these dimensions generally reflect Americans' biases toward meeting the needs of the nation through private efforts, individually (in a civil society) or, to a lesser degree, charitably (through the public dimension). Only if the first two dimensions do not meet an essential need, then Americans grudgingly accept governmental action. Government (state) action is called on only if the need is great and voluntary private efforts do not meet or sufficiently ameliorate the need. Government action, in general, is seen as coercive and an affront to liberty. For a Federalist, an activist government conveys the message to citizens that they are not responsible for the conditions of the nation. It sets up a separation, psychologically, if not in fact, between a citizenry in charge and the conditions facing the nation. It leads to a citizenry, therefore, hopelessly reduced to the whims of politics and politicians.

By providing the language of positive rights, do the Four Freedoms, in their attempt to provide protection from want and fear, simply equate to capitulation? Are they really a form of surrender to the realities of a modern, industrial, or postindustrial economy and to global markets? Or are they statements of a caring society, broadening the role of government to realistically meet the human necessities average people cannot meet for themselves?

Current Political Discourse

The Four Freedoms, two freedoms protecting negative rights and two freedoms protecting positive rights, can be seen as a transitional document. The Four Freedoms tie our established view of rights with a new view of rights that reflects the realities of an industrial and postindustrial world. The debate between conservatives (the prominent view of Republicans) and liberals (the prominent view of Democrats) can be seen as a continuum between two views: the federalist view and the Jacobist view. This is particularly true when considering economic issues. So basic are the biases of the federalist view and so real are the realities of the modern economy that neither the advocates of one side nor the advocates of the other can totally dismiss the language or substance of the opposing side. One can believe that even strong advocates for self initiative, conservatives, and those who support strong government intervention, liberals, share in the ideals of the other side. Conservatives often dismiss federalism's support of diversity and support a more nationalist view in terms of U.S. foreign policy and acceptance of international/global views of social and economic interests, while liberals find Federalist calls for an activist citizenry appealing. Read carefully the following excerpt from President George W. Bush's Second Inaugural Address:

> In America's ideal of freedom, citizens find the dignity and security of economic independence, instead of laboring on the edge of subsistence. This is the broader definition of liberty that motivated the Homestead Act, the Social Security Act, and the G.I. Bill of Rights. And now we will extend this vision by reforming great institutions to serve the needs of our time. To give every American a stake in the promise and future of our country, we will bring the highest standards to our schools, and build an ownership society. We will widen the ownership of homes and businesses, retirement savings and health

insurance—preparing our people for the challenges of life in a free society. By making every citizen an agent of his or her own destiny, we will give our fellow Americans greater *freedom from want and fear*, and make our society more prosperous and just and equal. (Bush, 2005, emphasis added)

Even this decidedly conservative politician pays homage to the language of the positive rights contained in the words "freedom from want and fear." In a turn of semantic logic, the president couches the freedoms, though, in terms of liberty, despite the coercive nature of government laws (we are all, at least, forced to pay taxes to support these programs) and adds notions of justice and equality only as afterthoughts. Some more liberally oriented advocates could couch these claims predominately in terms of justice. They might claim, due to the realities of current economic arrangements, that people cannot protect themselves fully from the vagaries of financial misfortune or secure those assets that promise a brighter future without the help of government. Therefore, justice demands that government provide the assistance represented by the programs the president listed. But if faced with the direct question of whether, as liberals or progressives, they are in favor of a citizenry that passively accepts government relieving them of their active participation or responsibility in providing for their own welfare, I doubt many would affirm such a view.

And what does the evidence show? Is there any evidence from recent American history or current conditions indicating that a more positive view of rights leads to a less engaged citizenry? Unfortunately, there is. Putnam (2000) writes in his extensive review of the relevant political science research, "Americans are playing virtually every aspect of the civic game less frequently today than we did two decades ago" (p. 41). In terms of voting, participating in civic organizations, communicating with policy makers, and the like, Americans have taken a more passive role. Gutierrez (2005), though, reports that adolescents express a bias toward "federalist" strategies in solving problems. That is, when given a choice between federalist strategies (getting as many stakeholders as possible involved) and other strategies (rule of the one, rule of the few, or "I'll do what I want to do" strategy), students overwhelmingly chose federalist options. So people who favor more communal approaches to civic concerns can take heart and see that, at least on an intellectual level, people do see the advantage of group action that presupposes they interact with others in solving mutual concerns.

The development of this debate or series of debates has had another consequence. As pointed out earlier, until the Great Depression, American traditional discourse was mostly issue centered. The general trend since then, but especially in the past ten–twenty years, has been for these debates to take on a more ideological bent. The diversity associated with federalist politics led to diverse interests coalescing and forming issue specific coalitions. An ally in one political fight could very well be an adversary in another fight. Today, the battle lines are becoming deeper and much more permanent.

Press accounts constantly report that it has become rare for politicians who find themselves on either side of this general divide to become friends or ever socialize together. An often repeated story after Republican President Reagan died was that during the 1980s when he was president, he would from time to time drink socially with then speaker of the House, Democrat Patrick "Tip" O'Neill. After the work of the day was done, they could be friends even though they were often political opponents. Today in Washington, reports indicate that adversaries enjoying each other's company in social settings have become almost nonexistent. The rhetoric has become sharper and personal. Often opponents question each other's patriotism, honesty, and character. Talk radio and cable news networks add to this type of political discourse.

Lasting Influence

There is no doubt that the language of the Four Freedoms was primarily aimed at the challenge posed by fascism and Nazism. Despite the strong isolationist feelings most Americans held prior to Pearl Harbor, once the nation was attacked, it readily fell in line with the war aims of Franklin Roosevelt. This included supporting the war against Germany, a nation that had not extensively "done" anything aggressive against the United States, beyond attacking a few of our war ships in the Atlantic and declaring war. There was no popular call for negotiating with Hitler before our active engagement began. One can interpret this development as an indication that FDR's propaganda, including the issuance of the Four Freedoms, worked and Americans came to understand and accept the menace to freedom that Hitler represented. The just experienced threat of the Great Depression and the threat posed by Hitler seemed encapsulated by the four statements defiantly claiming our rights against both sets of threats. The legacy of the Four Freedom includes many elements, among them a reflective document that posed the domestic debate for the subsequent years that have transpired.

References

Berlin, I. (1984). Two Concepts of Liberty. In M. Sandel (Ed.), *Liberalism and Its Critics* (pp. 15–36). New York: New York University Press.

Bush, G. W. (2005). Second inaugural address. http://www.whitehouse.gov/news/releases/2005/01/20050120–1.html, accessed June 23, 2005

Elazar, D. J. (1992). Lectures given at an institute at Steamboat Springs CO. Sponsored by the National Endowment for the Humanities.

Garraty, J. A. (1979). *The American Nation: A History of the United States*, 4th ed. New York: Harper and Row, Publishers.

Gutierrez, R. (2005). The Predisposition of High School Students to Engage in Collective Strategies of Problem-Solving. *Theory and Research in Social Education*. Accepted for publication. 33(3), 404–431

Morgan, T. (1985). *FDR: A biography*. New York: Touchstone.

Putnam, R. D. (2000). *Bowling Alone: The Collapse and Revival of American Community*. New York: Simon and Schuster.

Part II

Intellectual Perspectives on the Four Freedoms

The chapters in this section of *Educating for Democracy in a Changing World* deal with the philosophical and international perspectives of Roosevelt's Four Freedoms. In introducing this section, it is important in light of contemporary society to take a look at what freedom is. Each of these chapters questions the freedoms that the public believes and expects will be allotted to them as citizens. It is necessary to be vigilant to the limitations on alternatives and interpretation that can, in fact, under the guise of obeying, end up denying us our right to freedom of speech, religion, from want and fear. And, we have to be proactive as professionals, educators, as individuals and as part of the larger community to make sure that those in power make sure that these freedoms are protected and promoted.

Lesley Northup proposes that what we have now is a practice of the freedom of worship, of variety of faiths, rather than freedom of religion. This transformation has occurred as the result of a series of court cases that pit faith against science; vouchers to parochial schools; the teaching of evolution vs. creationism; in religious wars big and small; and in women's rights. There is an infusion of religion in our promise of protection by the government, in prayer, in rituals and community gatherings that promises a good life to those who acquiesce to the state. The protection of freedom of worship is now the business of government rather than the promise of freedom of religion from government influence.

Pablo Toral provides a global perspective to the needs of underdeveloped, poor countries and the global environmental dangers of unchecked growth, environmental abuse, and disease. The freedom that he relates to is that of want, and he directs our attention to unchecked growth and economic expansion at the expense of certain countries for the financial advancement of multinational corporations that make the rules of the game of success. Left behind are those countries and the people in them that are denied human rights, peace, democracy, and security, and food, clothing, shelter and competitive skills in the global marketplace.

Louis and Ann Marie Pagliaro suggest that freedom is an inherent desire and that in order for liberty, and its correlate freedom, to flourish we need to abolish fear. This can be done by defending freedom and by supporting conditions necessary to achieve that end. Peace and happiness are dependent on freedom from fear—from terrorism—and courage is needed along with personal determination to do whatever needs to be done along with a government that is committed not to the fight, but to the freedoms that they are defending.

Steven Selden exposes another attack on our freedoms, that of the conservative challenge to take over the undergraduate curriculum by partisan advisory bodies that infuse a particular ideological focus to the open forum of ideas that is the promise of the university experience. The freedom from coercion, the promise of a university education, is in fact influenced largely by an agenda that supports a market driven creation of persons able to fit into the economic realities of special interest groups, corporations, foundations and politicos. In the quest for traditional knowledge, the culture wars have escalated from the content of the curriculum to the process of higher education that molds and shapes a particular point of view.

4

The First Amendment, the Second Freedom, and the Third Millennium

LESLEY A. NORTHRUP

Sixty-five percent
—AVERAGE NUMBER OF FIRST-YEAR STUDENTS IN MY CLASSES WHO AGREE WITH THE STATEMENT, "IT IS ONLY FAIR TO TEACH CREATIONISM ALONGSIDE EVOLUTION."

A significant number of my first-year college students in cosmopolitan Miami think the Bible gives a more accurate account of the source of life than does evolutionary science. A smaller number have given up religion altogether because they cannot reconcile their parents' faith with their adolescent version of rational thought. And a solid majority think it is "only fair" that evolution and creationism—no more than competing "theories" in their estimation—should both be taught in school so students can make up their own minds on the matter. Queried further, my students consistently advert to the constitutional guarantee of freedom of religion: "Hey, everyone's got the right to believe whatever they want." Their understanding of freedom of religion, American style, is the current version of an intellectual construct that has changed, radically and constantly, throughout the country's history.

The First Amendment on Religion: A Brief Refresher

That there is a constitutional freedom of religion is largely attributable, in its original form, to James Madison. As we all know, the early English colonists were not particularly interested in religious freedom, except for themselves; the Massachusetts Bay colony, for example, was famously intolerant of all but the purest Puritans. With land enough for each community to set up shop on its own, the notion that pluralistic religious beliefs could be a positive societal force flourished in but a few locations, and at the time of the Revolution, nine of thirteen colonies had established state religious institutions. By 1776, the one-size-fits-all notion of an official state religion had not changed much since Americans were English.

After independence, the constitution proposed by Madison required unanimous approval, which he knew he could not achieve with an embedded bill of rights; Jefferson and others, however, were convinced that individuals and non-majority groups needed protection, especially for religious freedom. Ardent anti-federalists, themselves opposed to guaranteed rights, used the absence of such assurances in the proposed document as a political excuse to try to scuttle the whole project, while democrats demanded that they be included. As a compromise, Madison secured a promise from the Constitutional Congress to consider them after ratification, and the constitution was passed in 1787. The Bill of Rights drafted and stage-managed by Madison and accepted by an ideologically weary Congress two years later protected dissenting beliefs and their expression from the twin tyrannies of federal government and majority rule.

Encapsulated in the first of the ten amendments in the Bill were the liberties that today we accept as projecting the country's ethos: freedom of religion, speech, assembly, and the press. The pithy definition of freedom of religion comprises two clauses: "Government shall make no law respecting an establishment of religion or prohibiting the free exercise thereof." A great deal of jurisprudence since that time has been devoted to defining and refining those two clauses—one preventing the government from forcing conformance with any one religion, the other allowing all religions to flourish—largely with reference to a mysterious datum termed "original intent." This supposedly accessible artifact represents the mindset held toward the Bill by "the framers," an equally indefinable notion that comprises either Jefferson, Madison, and other free-thinking federalists, if you are a liberal, or, if you are a conservative, the politicians that fought both union and any restriction whatsoever on the behavior of the states. Depending on the changing tides of political fortune, the original intent of the framers is variously interpreted as (1) an anticipation that times, needs, governments, and peoples change and require a flexible structure, or (2) the absolute minimum of lawmaking that the wording of the document allows.

The original intent of some personages important to the process is, in fact, not that difficult to determine. Madison initially thought a bill of rights to be unnecessary and limiting, but changed his mind, at least partly at Jefferson's urging. Having done so, he became a politically astute and fervent believer in the need to protect the minority from the majority. The original intent of those opposing the amendments was primarily to use debate over them as a wedge to gut the authority of the new federal government. The original intent of just about everyone seems to be that the government would never need to say anything about religion at all. Whether it matters one whit what these people may have been mulling over in their heart of hearts is another question altogether.

Even as the ink was drying on the first ten amendments, arguments about the original meaning of freedom of religion flourished, and attempts were made to further amend the constitution to clarify this key concept. In 1864, the National Reform Association, believing the Civil War to have demonstrated God's judgment on an irreligious country, proposed a "Christian Amendment," adding language to the preamble of the constitution "recognizing the being and attributes of Almighty God, the Divine Authority of the Holy Scriptures, the law of God as the paramount rule, and Jesus, the Messiah, the Savior and Lord of all." This proposal, which would of course have made Christianity the official religion of the country and the foundation of its law and ethics, had a surprisingly long run, though ultimately it was not adopted. At the other end of the spectrum, the Cincinnati schools decision of 1873, declaring, in essence, that public schools could not teach religion, led to the Blaine School Amendment, which sought to make explicit the wall of separation between church and state. Shortly afterward, Congress rejected both these amendments, wisely leaving freedom of religion flexible and loosely defined. It has remained in that fruitful limbo since then.

FDR's Second Freedom: Freedom of Worship

In his eloquent Four Freedoms State of the Union address in 1941, Franklin Delano Roosevelt reiterated "those things [that] have toughened the fiber of our people, have renewed their faith and strengthened their devotion to the institutions we make ready to protect." This inspirational wartime rhetoric announced common agreement on what Robert Bellah, adopting a term from Rousseau, has called "American Civil Religion."[1] As described by him and countless subsequent religion scholars, this unique feature of American life makes continual reference to the nation's original self-understanding as having been singularly blessed by God for a holy purpose, and to the deist vision of Jefferson and other early Americans, which eschewed any particular faith while casting a Protestant hue over the country's goals, achievements, and values. Like every president before or since, FDR alluded to this amorphous vision of special favor and purpose in the eyes of the Almighty that lay like a blanket of good fortune across the United States.

Its practical application was the set of freedoms he invoked, brilliantly linking hallowed portions of the country's foundational document with the hallmarks of his

New Deal, and foreshadowing the Universal Declaration of Human Rights engineered by first lady Eleanor Roosevelt in 1948. Unlike freedom from want and from fear (necessary but unique features of his own agenda), the first two freedoms he listed, of speech and "of every person to worship God in his own way—everywhere in the world," required no elaboration and were simply stated as given and understood by all. Freedom of religion had become, in the words of "The United Nations Fight for the Four Freedoms," a pamphlet published by the Office of War Information in 1942, "part of our soil and of the sky above this continent."

However, FDR's speech does not actually advert to freedom of religion. Instead it cites freedom of *worship*. Generally, we do not stop to ponder the distinctions between these terms, but the changing language reflects changing approaches to the First Amendment that mirrored national cultural shifts. It can be argued—and has been, at length—that Roosevelt, in specifying worship rather than religion, deliberately referred to freedom of practice, not just of thought—to the right not only to believe as one chooses, but also to express those beliefs in action.

It is as difficult to know Roosevelt's original intent as that of the founders, but it seems likely he chose his words carefully. If so, this peculiar distinction reflects the religious landscape of the twentieth century, vastly more diverse than that of the late eighteenth century. What most required protection in the 1940s was variety of religious expression, not of religious belief. The countless new religions of the 1800s had led to widespread acceptance that, for good or ill, beliefs of all sorts were proliferating and demanded tolerance; there was little debate any longer about the need for freedom of belief. On the other hand, issues of religious practice were on the table, hot and ready to eat, especially as massive immigration exposed traditionally Protestant Americans to menus of religious action they could scarcely stomach.

In articulating his Second Freedom, Roosevelt, himself a mainline Episcopalian, would have had in mind, primarily, the minor differences in worship habits of other mainline denominations—Presbyterians, Lutherans, Disciples of Christ, and so on—and perhaps those of Roman Catholics and Jews, but he would also have had to take into account the behaviors of the Buddhist Chinese who helped settle the West, the spiritualists who had flourished in the wake of the Civil War, the Christian Scientists and other transcendental thinkers of the early 1900s, and an influx of Hindus, among other new practices. All these religions were permitted to arrive, thrive, and adapt on U.S. shores, having been granted freedom of religion by the constitution. The question at hand, however, was whether any public practice, no matter how offensive or dangerous, was similarly protected.

Religion inherently fosters two kinds of action: ethical behavior and ritual. In the United States, religious ethics has folded itself neatly into Civil Religion—witness the current argument over the place of the Ten Commandments in the nation's legal code. What are commonly referred to as "family values" or, more broadly, American values, are the essential tenets of Protestant Christianity, adopted into Reform Judaism and other American versions of world religions, and sprinkled with a healthy dose of humanism. In mid-century, there was little disagreement about these ethical principles, which were brought into even clearer focus with the rising threat of Hitler.

Not surprisingly, certain religious behaviors offended common ethical standards, and raised the awkward problem of whether the government, while granting freedom to believe and to theorize about belief, could nonetheless curtail the right to particular religious practices. In the most obvious example, in 1879, the Supreme Court ruled that polygamy was prohibited, despite the strongly held (and protected) beliefs of Mormons. The Court at that time noted that although laws "cannot interfere with mere religious beliefs and opinions, they may with practices."[2] Additional cases against Mormon sects practicing plural marriage were adjudicated throughout the 1940s.[3] Similarly, in 1940, the Court ruled that Jehovah's Witnesses were required to do their patriotic duty and salute the flag, against their belief that this constituted idolatry.[4]

Thus, while matters of belief had created complex court cases, worship practices were increasingly likely to run afoul of governmental interests. In 1942, the Holiness Church was required to obey a statute forbidding snakes "in connection with any religious service," effectively outlawing its central act of worship.[5] As the Court had said in 1890, "It was never intended or supposed that the Amendment could be invoked as a protection against legislation for the punishment of acts inimical to the peace, good order and morals of society. . . . However free the exercise of religion may be, it must be subordinate to the criminal laws of the country."[6]

In his speech, Roosevelt appeared to take the position that worship practices should be, generally, protected as well as beliefs. Whether or not Roosevelt consciously sought to expand the definition of freedom of religion by including freedom of worship, the Four Freedoms speech marked a broadening in the country's understanding of that quintessential right.

Freedom of Religion after Roosevelt

Like Roosevelt's speech, the 1942 booklet on the United Nations and the Four Freedoms does not name freedom of religion as crucial to the nation's ethos. But it does not speak of freedom of worship, either. Rather, it claims freedom of *conscience* as that precious ideal rooted in our lands and heavens. This is a significant further construction of religious rights, carried forward in the 1948 Universal Declaration of Human Rights, which reads in Article 18:

Everyone has the right to freedom of thought, conscience and religion; this right includes freedom to change his religion or belief, and freedom, either alone or in community with others and in public or private, to manifest his religion or belief in teaching, practice, worship and observance.

Here, freedom of religion is linked with freedom of thought *and* conscience, and further defined as freedom of both belief and its expression in worship. This expanded understanding of freedom of religion, ironically, returns us to the true "original intent" of at least some key founders, who no doubt would have been pleased to see that, after 200 years, their convictions were being honored. Madison had written that "the Religion then of every man must be left to the conviction and conscience of every man,"[7] and Jefferson had "sworn upon the altar of God eternal hostility against every form of tyranny over the mind of man."[8] The evolution of freedom of religion to include a freedom of conscience that transcended mere ecclesiastical alliances and even outward expressions of faith would surely have pleased these two champions of liberty.

A classic example involves those whose conscience forbids them to bear arms. Even before the Revolution, the First Continental Congress had recognized this problem, especially with regard to Quakers and Moravians; members debated whether it was reasonable to expect those who would fight to defend those who would not, and some suggested that conscientious objectors should compensate the government financially for their nonparticipation. In the event, it was decided to leave the matter flexible, since it was almost impossible to word an exemption unambiguously. In 1917, the Selective Service Act exempted from combat members of "any well-recognized religious sect or organization," defining conscientious objector status by institutional affiliation. In 1940, reflecting the broadened understanding of freedom of conscience, the Selective Draft Act specifically exempted from combat persons who, "by reason of religious training or belief," would not fight, abandoning the requirement of membership in particular religious groups.

It is worth noting that the 1948 Declaration also substantially elaborates freedom of worship as inclusive of freedom of action, individually or communally, in public or in private, in pedagogy and in praxis. This expanded redefinition is all the more significant because the charter assumes it applies to all nations, whereas previously it had been thought to be solely the province of the United States and those few other countries where freedom of religion was constitutionalized. Indeed, even today many nations, including some in the United Nations, give lip service to the idea but have difficulty implementing a notion essentially incompatible with their cultural history.

From Roosevelt's day to the end of the century, U.S. First Amendment case law burgeoned. Free exercise challenges to freedom of conscience continued, resulting in rulings that, for example, allowed the Amish to exempt their children from public schooling[9] and affirmed the employment rights of Sabbath observers.[10] Meanwhile, the precedence of public-interest laws over worship practices was affirmed with regard to, for example, the Native American use of peyote in religious rituals[11] and modified slightly with reference to animal sacrifice in Santeria worship.[12]

Despite these developments in free exercise theory, the predominant focus shifted in this period to applications of the establishment clause, as questions of the separation of church and state assumed major importance. Among the many key establishment issues considered in the last half-century—IRS exemptions for religious organizations, draft evasion, religious solicitation, Sunday closing ("blue") laws, among others—some thirty or forty crucial cases dealt with the convoluted questions of religious liberty and public education, as the constitutionally permissible entanglement of tax-supported schools and religious expression was adjudicated. Among the issues decided in this area were the legitimacy of public assistance to and vouchers for parochial schools, prayer in public schools, and religious instruction in the public classroom.

In that eventful half-century, the Supreme Court defined the standard for the separation of church and state in the landmark *Lemon* case, striking down state assistance to private schools: A statute must, it said, have a secular legislative purpose; neither advance nor inhibit religion; and avoid fostering an "excessive entanglement of government with religion."[13] In applying this standard, the courts generally have been more liberal with faith-based social service agencies than with schools, and more liberal with higher education than with elementary and secondary education, applying in the case of the latter a "bright line" separating the situation of children from that of adults. In practice, this reflects a judgment that children are more vulnerable to religious proselytizing than their elders and require further protection from it.

In the 1980s and 1990s, the rise of the Religious Right, that astonishing mixture of faith and politics championing conservative ideology, pushed to the forefront a judicial agenda with the unapologetic goal of injecting religion into both the public square and the public schools. A key goal was to position religious conservatives as majorities on public school boards throughout the country in order to control curriculum and religious expression in public schools, an endeavor which was very successful, at least at first. In November of 1993, *Time* magazine reported that conservative Christian candidates won about 40% of the more than 500 races they entered in 1992, often by failing to reveal their position on religious issues, and that they "monopolized many school agendas with challenges that say more about the parents' political and religious beliefs than their children's education." Among their key goals were restoring prayer in the schools, allowing religious after-school activities, and teaching the Bible and creationism.

These latter two curricular initiatives met with divergent fates in the courts. Teaching the Bible in K-12, especially as religion or history, was consistently rejected, though teaching it in higher education—where students could contextualize it within specific disciplines, such as literature or religious studies, has been relatively uncontroversial. In 1994, the Supreme Court ruled that a Bible course in Mississippi public schools was unconstitutional,[14] and shortly after, a similar course in Florida met the same fate. In 1999, the Georgia Board of Education announced it would no longer fund Bible courses, and the battle shifted to Tennessee, where such courses were also ruled unconstitutional in 2002.

The second curricular goal of the movement, following a 1987 Supreme Court decision[15] forbidding states to require that creationism be taught along with evolution, was replacing or supplementing science courses in public schools with "creation science"—later called "intelligent design"—the biblical creation account dressed in the garb of empiricism. The strategy was multi-pronged: tout creationism as truly scientific; threaten boycotts of textbook publishers to force changes in their materials on evolution; and appeal to that pervasive sense of fairness engrained in the American consciousness with a dumbed-down distortion of the idea of protecting the rights of the minority to freedom of expression. Amid many successes with this strategy, the end of the century saw the beginning of a backlash against it: In 1999, Kansas abandoned an attempt to minimize evolution in its science curriculum in the face of public ridicule rather than judicial activism, as its conservative school board members failed to be reelected. Nonetheless, the trumpeting of the dubious "fairness" standard by today's students is more an indicator of the success of the Right's public relations campaign than of any rational consideration on the part of our young people.

The movement fared better on the legal front with a series of initiatives to allow funding of K-12 religious schools via tax-backed vouchers. Such programs, enacted in numerous localities, were vindicated in large part in 2000 by a Supreme Court decision that declared, in essence, that diverting public funds to religious-school tuition was not inherently unconstitutional.[16]

On the other hand, rulings on prayer in schools generally were negative. From 1962's landmark *Engel v. Vitale* ruling[17] that such prayer was unconstitutional, a barrage of cases was brought by conservatives, testing every conceivable variation on the idea: The courts have held firm, however, that any form of sanctioned prayer among public schoolchildren violates the separation of church and state.[18]

Despite such setbacks, the continued pressure from the Right to put religion in the schools led to the passage in 1993 of the Religious Freedom Protection Act (RFPA), allowing great latitude in public support of religion; the RFPA, however, failed constitutional scrutiny in 1997. This ruling infuriated conservatives, leading to the proposal of a sweeping constitutional amendment aimed at destroying the longstanding division of church and state. The proposed 1995 Religious Freedom Amendment (RFA) promised that, among other things, "neither the United States nor any State shall abridge the freedom of any person or group, including students in public schools, to engage in prayer or other religious expression."

The RFA failed to be enacted, but in the same year a consolation prize was adopted—a set of federal guidelines encouraging partnerships between schools and religious agencies to promote ethical behavior, safety, and discipline; these were endorsed by President Clinton, who said schools should not be "religion-free zones." His remark gave voice to yet another aspect of the simmering dispute—the argument that "freedom of religion should not mean freedom *from* religion." The Right has demanded that freedom of religion must apply anywhere, everywhere— including in public places at taxpayer expense, arguing that the founders' original intent had never been to ban the public expression of religion, specifically of Christian Protestantism. The countervailing argument, which has held, tenuously, in the judiciary, has been that the minority—non-Christians and/or atheists— cannot be compelled to either subsidize or attend to prayer in public schools. As the country entered the third millennium, only a fragile judicial balance maintained this interpretation of the First Amendment.

The Third Millennium

The September 11 terrorist attacks on U.S. targets raised new concerns about freedom of religion. Questions without answers—religious questions—abounded: Was this an attack of one religion against another? Were Muslims incited to violence by their religious beliefs? Did Islam want to take over the United States? Were we harboring terrorists in U.S. mosques? Should Islam be allowed to flourish here?

Cherished notions of freedom and security, good and evil, fate and destiny underwent immediate and transformative reevaluation on that day. Above all, for many, the attack was at its core a religious statement and more—an affront, a challenge to the heart of American faith. "This war is fundamentally religious," Osama bin Laden said. "The enmity is based on creed.... It is a question of faith.... They know they are right and they resist the most ferocious, serious, and violent Crusade campaign against Islam ever since the message was revealed to Muhammad," he said, arguing that Western Christianity, led by the United States, is waging a systematic religious war against Islam. Scholars and imams stressed that the Islam of the Q'uran is a religion of peace, and described the terrorists as extremist and debased. Nonetheless, well-known Muslim author Salmon Rushdie was clear that "Yes, this is about Islam" (New *York Times,* November 2, 2001), noting that Muslim societies do not, in fact, live by the pure theology of the Q'uran.[19]

For the United States, despite repeated assertions to the contrary, the response to the attacks was also largely about religion. Among President Bush's first acts was to declare a national day of prayer. In public speaking, he routinely asked God to watch over America, and intoned, "God Bless America" at the end of every talk. His speech to the United Nations on November 10 unapologetically used the language of religion: "We are confident, too, that history has an Author, Who fills time and eternity with His purpose. We know that evil is real, but good will prevail against it. This is the teaching of many faiths." Then Bush called his reactive war on terrorism a "crusade," just as bin Laden had.

Evangelists like Jerry Falwell pronounced the attacks God's retribution. Falwell said they were "probably what we deserve," specifically blaming gays and lesbians, abortion providers, liberal advocacy groups, and "all of them who have tried to secularize America." "You helped this happen," he thundered, by prompting God to remove his "protective hand."

If the attacks were fraught with religious significance, one effect was to demonstrate just how little Americans knew and understood about Islam. The media moved into the void, writing voluminously about the religion and its teachings. The flood of information, and the general concern that Muslims be treated fairly, led to a surprisingly gentle attitude toward American Muslims overall. In an ABCNews/Beliefnet survey taken in October, 47% of Americans said they viewed Islam favorably. People seemed genuinely interested to learn of the religion's many advances in areas as disparate as science, women's economic independence, and philosophy.

All this highlighted the iconic power of the First Amendment even in the most adverse circumstances. Despite the widespread perception that the attacks were religious in nature and the blaringly religious U.S. response, Americans as a whole continued to respect the principle that everyone, no matter how suspect, is entitled to his own religious beliefs and worship. If any aspect of the expanded understanding of the first freedom seemed newly called into question, it was freedom of conscience; while the attacks might not have been about pure or even traditional Islam, nor about Muslim worship, it seemed rather clear that they *were* about the conscientious, if twisted, *application* of faith by Islamic militants. The long-term response of the U.S. government, interning large numbers of Muslims at Guantanamo—most of them clearly prisoners of conscience, not action—indicated just how far the country was willing to go to clip "conscience" from the definition imbedded in the UN Declaration.

If the importance of the free exercise clause came into focus as Americans extended it even to the Muslims among them, the establishment clause suffered further erosion as a consequence of 9/11. The wall between church and state, though under severe attack, had remained steadfast throughout the end of the twentieth century, guaranteeing that majority Protestant Americans could not completely dominate schools, elections, and the public square. In the religious flush that followed the attacks, when invocations of the Almighty became frequent, no one seemed disposed to point to the church-state wall.

In October, *Time* magazine noted that, while prayer and religious symbols adorned school and governmental gatherings, "No one is protesting yet." A high school principal in Florida enthused that "my students and employees have been praying openly, and now it isn't questioned." Born-again evangelical Jay Sekulow of the conservative American Center for Law and Justice talked of a "real swelling up of civic religion" that could have a pronounced impact on the future of constitutional law. The substitution of "God Bless America" for the national anthem at sporting events prompted widespread suggestions that it be a permanent replacement.

Still, the wall has stood. In today's climate, that elusive construct, original intent, raises its battered head more stubbornly than ever before, as advocates of judicial restraint argue against the interpretive powers of the judiciary. While other rallying cries of the Religious Right have fallen aside as too shrill or too insupportable, the call for strict judicial construction of the constitution remains compelling, and underlies the battles over Supreme Court appointments that have dominated the second term of George Bush the younger. As Bush's appointees take their places, there is widespread concern that the moderate center that had balanced the Court through the last three decades would give way to an ideologically conservative majority that would allow religious concepts to dominate the law in such critical areas as abortion rights, the application of scientific advances, unlimited detainment of suspected Muslim "terrorists," and public support of religious education.

Conclusion

In his Four Freedoms speech, FDR considered each of the freedoms as vitally necessary not only to personal liberty but also to the progress of the country and of the human person: "Give them to him in full and abundant measure and he will cross the threshold of a new age, the greatest age of man." The War Department booklet elaborated on that theme as well: "In the design for a new and better world, religious freedom is a fundamental prop." Of all the beliefs of American Civil Religion, perhaps this is the most aboriginal and unfaltering—the notion that the New Israel, specially anointed by God, will go from strength to strength into an ever-brightening future. Of course, FDR spoke before Hiroshima, before Vietnam, before the religious wars of the late twentieth century, before 9/11. Still, this central tenet captures the heart of the United States, the nation that British theologian commentator G.K. Chesterton once called the "country with the soul of a church."

The genius of Jefferson, Madison, and the other founders was specifically avoiding writing their own intentions into the constitution, leaving a flexible, living document that could go forward into the future as the country grew in stature and took an international leadership role. Original intent, that rallying cry of the Right, is lost (as it should be) with the original intenders. What they left instead in the First Amendment is a resounding yet pliable statement on religious freedom that fits the twenty-first century as neatly as it did the eighteenth.

That statement has evolved to recognize that religion is more than belief, more than worship, more than ethical laws. Religion is the conscience of the individual in community, the rituals that invoke greater meaning in our lives, the conceptions, and practices—however alien, however shocking—that shape our convictions. And, according to our constitution and every one of our greatest leaders, it is only the business of government when it needs protection.

Notes

1. Robert Bellah, "Civil Religion in America," reprinted in *Beyond Belief: Essays on Religion in a Post-traditional World*, New York: Harper and Row, 1970, pp. 168–189.
2. *Reynolds v. United States*, 98 U.S. 145, 166 (1878).
3. For example, *United States v. Barlow*, 56 F. Supp. 795 (D. Utah 1944) and *Cleveland v. United States*, 329 U.S. 14 (1946).
4. *Minersville School District v. Gobitis*, 310 U.S. 586 (1940). This came at the same time the Court reversed an earlier ruling and said that Jehovah's Witnesses could not be prevented from distributing literature, a mandated action in their religion, under statutes forbidding disturbing the peace. (*Cantwell v. Connecticut*, 310 U.S. 296 [1940]). Again, the Court emphasized that Free Exercise "embraces two concepts—freedom to believe and freedom to act. The first is absolute, but in the nature of things, the second cannot be." This ruling was overturned three years later in *West Virginia Board of Education v. Barnette*, 319 U.S. 624 (1943).
5. *Accord Lawson v. Commonwealth*, 291 Ky. 437, 164 S.W. 2nd 927 (1942).
6. *Davis v. Beason*, 133 U.S. at 342. The principle thus established led, after the famous ruling in *Employment Division v. Smith*, 494 U.S. 872 (1990) ruling, in effect, that use of peyote by members of the Native American Church could be regulated by government antidrug law, to the passage of the Religious Freedom Restoration Act of 1993, which went so far in protecting religious freedom that it was itself overruled by the court in *Boerne v. Flores*, 73 F. 3rd 1352 (1997). The much less sweeping Religious Land Use and Institutionalized Persons Act was enacted in 2000.
7. Papers of James Madison, 8:299. A. A. Lipscomb, ed., *Writings of Thomas Jefferson*, Washington, D.C.: Thomas 8. Jefferson Memorial Association, 1903, Vol. 10, p. 175.
9. *Wisconsin v. Yoder*, 406 U.S. 205 (1972).
10. *Sherbert v. Verner*, 374 U.S. 398 (1963).

11. See note 6.
12. *Church of the Lukumi Babalu Aye v. City of Hialeah*, 508 U.S. 520 (1993).
13. *Lemon v. Kurtzman*, 403 U.S. 602 (1971).
14. *Herdahl v. Pontotoc Co. School District*.
15. *Edwards v. Aguillard*, 482 U.S. 578 (1987).
16. *Zelman v. Simmons-Harris*.
17. 370 U.S. 421 (1962).
18. *Abington Township v. Schempp*, 374 U.S. 203 (1963); *Wallace v. Jaffree*, 472 U.S. 38 (1985), et al.
19. Some of the material in this section was presented somewhat differently in Lesley A. Northup, "Islam and the New World," *Diversity Exchange* (Spring 2002), pp. 28–29.

5
Four Freedoms in a Global Context

PABLO TORAL

On September 8, 2000, the General Assembly of the United Nations adopted the "United Nations Millennium Declaration." The governments represented at the General Assembly decided to strive to advance eight main goals: the reaffirmation of faith in the values and principles of the UN Charter; peace, security and disarmament; development and poverty eradication; environmental protection; human rights, democracy and good governance; protecting the vulnerable; meeting the special needs of Africa; and strengthening the United Nations.[1] To achieve these goals, the UN sponsored the "United Nations Millennium Project" under the guidance of Jeffrey D. Sachs. The project estimates that, if its recommendations are implemented successfully, 500 million people will be lifted out of extreme poverty in 2015, 300 million will no longer suffer hunger, the lives of 2 million mothers will be saved, 30 million children will be saved from dying before reaching their fifth birthday, 350 million people will gain access to safe drinking water and 650 million will gain access to basic sanitation.[2]

The UN Millennium Declaration and the UN Millennium Project follow the spirit of F. D. Roosevelt's Four Freedoms speech, in which he called for a world founded upon four essential freedoms: freedom of speech and expression, freedom to worship God, freedom from want, and freedom from fear.[3] In this chapter I will review some of the challenges the international community faces today to advance the goals included in the UN Millennium Project before 2015 and evaluate our ability to create a world that realizes F. D. Roosevelt's Four Freedoms. I argue that to succeed in the implementation of every point of the declaration and the project, the international community needs to address some fundamental challenges that threaten to make these two documents just another formulation of good intentions with little practical implications for the achievement of a just world.

Peace, Security and Disarmament

> We will spare no effort to free our peoples from the scourge of war, whether within or between States, which has claimed more than 5 million lives in the past decade. We will also seek to eliminate the dangers posed by weapons of mass destruction.[4]

Several important international treaties have been signed to achieve peace and security in the world in the modern era. The Treaty of Westphalia (1648), the Hague Conventions for the Pacific Settlement of International Disputes (1899, 1907), the Kellogg-Briand Pact renouncing the use of war for the solution of international controversies (1928) and the UN Charter (1945) have been some of the more important legal documents observed in the conduct of interstate relations.[5] However, these legal bodies have not succeeded in eliminating the use of force. Zbigniew Brzezinski estimates that the number of "lives deliberately extinguished by politically motivated carnage" in the twentieth century until 1990 was between 167 million and 175 million. These included 87,500,000 war dead (33,500,000 military war dead and 54,000,000 civilian war dead) and 80 million not-war dead (60 million resulting from communist oppression).[6] In the ten most deadly conflicts initiated in the 1990s alone the number of war dead ranged from 1,440,000 to 7,370,000[7] (see table 5.1) and in the twenty-first century several armed conflicts continued to claim the lives of thousands of people: Israel-Palestine, the Darfur Crisis in Sudan, Afghanistan and Iraq are just reminders that peace and security are still elusive goals in many parts of the world.

TABLE 5.1. Estimated Number of Deaths in the Ten Deadliest Conflicts Initiated in the 1990s

Conflict	Years	Estimated number of deaths (range)
Rwanda	1994	500,000–1,000,000
Angola	1992–1994	100,000–500,000
Somalia	1991–1999	48,000–300,000
Bosnia	1992–1995	35,000–250,000

Continued on the next page

Liberia	1991–1996	25,000–200,000
Burundi	1993	30,000–200,000
Chechnya	1994–1996	30,000–90,000
Tajikistan	1992–1999	30,000–100,000
Algeria	1992–1999	30,000–100,000
Gulf War	1990–1991	4,300–100,000

Source: Murray, C. J. L., King, G., López, A. D., Tomijima, N., and Grug, E. G. (2002), "Armed Conflict as a Public Health Problem," *BMH*, 321 (February), pp. 346–349.

The destructive power of nuclear weapons increases the likelihood that future international conflicts might cause large numbers of dead. Experts are split on the role that nuclear weapons play in conflict prevention. Realist scholars of international politics such as Kenneth Waltz believe that the spread of nuclear weapons are the best instrument to eliminate armed conflict. He believes that the destructive potential of these weapons forces governments that possess nuclear weapons to seek peaceful ways to settle disputes, given the potential high cost of using nuclear weapons.[8] Other scholars such as Robert Keohane and Joseph Nye question the usefulness of weapons (nuclear and nonnuclear) in the conduct of international relations, and argue that the self-interest that emerges from economic relations is the best guarantor of international peace and security. Keohane and Nye believe that through economic exchange governments and societies realize that they need one another and therefore they are likely to cooperate.[9] In spite of its 188 signatories, the Treaty of Non-Proliferation of Nuclear Weapons (1968) has been unable to deter some countries from developing nuclear warheads. In 2005, the "nuclear club" included nine countries (see table 5.2).

TABLE 5.2. Nuclear Warheads in 2005

Country	Nuclear warheads
Russia	16,000
USA	10,350
China	400
France	350
UK	200
Israel	100–200
Pakistan	40–60
India	40–50
North Korea	6–8

Source: Natural Resources Defense Council.

The achievement of peace and security requires the elimination of the sources of conflict as well as the means to wage armed conflict.[10] The US invasion of Iraq in 2003 represented a great challenge for international peace and security because it was a violation of international law. Chapter VI, Article 2 (3) of the UN Charter obliges member states to "settle their disputes by peaceful means in such a manner that international peace and security, and justice, are not endangered." Chapter VII, entitled "Action with respect to threats to the peace, breaches of the peace and acts of aggression," in article 40 gives the Security Council the power to establish measures to prevent threats to peace, breaches of peace and acts of aggression. Article 41 provides for binding nonmilitary enforcement action, such as "complete or partial interruption of economic relations and of rail, sea, air, postal, telegraphic, radio, and other means of communication, and the severance of diplomatic relations." Article 42 specifies that if actions taken under article 41 were inadequate, the Security Council "may take such action by air, sea, or land forces as may be necessary to maintain or restore international peace and security."[11]

Apart from the loss of human lives and suffering, the US invasion of Iraq has generated a huge cost to the United States, both economically and in terms of public image overseas. Although Americans see themselves as a "shining city on a hill," there is widespread hostility to the United States in the Arab and Muslim world, and China, Russia, India, the European Union, among other actors, have accused the United States of ignoring their interests in its pursuit of foreign policy. Stephen M. Walt concludes that the United States should involve itself in "fixing" failed states such as Afghanistan, Liberia, Rwanda, Sierra Leone or Somalia not just on humanitarian grounds, because they can affect the national security of the United States since they can become a breeding ground for terrorist organizations. He also points out that the United States "cannot go it alone," and instead recommends the US government to build an international coalition to advance four main policy areas: antiterrorism, enhancing control over weapons of mass destruction, reconstructing Afghanistan (and failed states), and rebuilding relations with the Arab and Muslim world.[12] The United Nations can be the forum to channel these policy goals, bringing together the international community.

Development and Poverty Eradication

> We will spare no effort to free our fellow men, women and children from the abject and dehumanizing conditions of extreme poverty, to which more than a billion of them are currently subjected. We are committed to making the right to development a reality for everyone and to freeing the entire human race from want.[13]

The "United Nations Millennium Project" makes the achievement of sustained rates of economic growth the core of its strategy. The project makes a direct connection between capital accumulation and economic growth on the one hand, and the alleviation of hunger, education, gender equality and health, on the other. All forms of capital are interrelated and contribute to economic growth which, in turn, contributes to the development of all kinds of capital: business capital, social capital, human capital, infrastructure, knowledge capital, natural capital and public institutional capital.[14]

To be successful in the achievement of these goals, the project will need to pay attention to those areas where action is needed more urgently. Table 5.3 shows that GDP and GDP per capita only grew significantly above the high income countries in South and East Asia between 1975 and 2001. In the low and middle-income regions of Europe and Central Asia and in Sub-Saharan Africa economic growth could not compensate for the growth in population, resulting in net reductions of GDP per capita. In the Arab countries GDP growth per capita stayed below 1% annually (see tables 5.3 and 5.4).

The share of population living in extreme poverty increased between 1990 and 2001 in Eastern Europe and Central Asia, in North Africa and the Middle East, as well as in Sub-Saharan Africa. In Latin America and the Caribbean it only dropped between 9% and 10% and only in South and East Asia it has fallen considerably. More than three quarters of the population of Sub-Saharan Africa and South Asia lived with less than $2.15 a day in 2001, almost half the population of East Asia, and one fifth of the population of Eastern Europe and Central Asia (see table 5.5).

TABLE 5.3. World GDP Growth, 1980–2001

	Annual GDP growth		Per capita GDP growth	
	1980–1990	1990–2000	1975–2001	1990–2001
World	3.2	2.6	1.2	1.2
Low income	4.4	4.7	1.6	1.4
Middle income	3.2	3.3	1.6	2.2
Lower middle income	4.0	3.4	-	-
Upper middle income	2.5	3.0	-	-
Low and middle income	3.4	3.4	2.3	2.9
East Asia and Pacific	8.0	7.2	5.9	5.5
Europe and Central Asia	2.4	0.2	-2.5	-1.6
Latin Am. & Caribbean	1.7	2.7	0.7	1.5
Arab states	2.0	3.2	0.3	0.7
South Asia	5.7	5.5	2.4	3.2
Sub-Saharan Africa	1.7	2.7	-0.9	-0.1
High Income	3.1	2.5	2.1	1.7

Source: World Bank (2005), World Development Report, p. 261; (2000/2001), pp. 295, 315; UNDP, Human Development Report 2003. MDGs: A Compact Among Nations to End Human Poverty, p. 281.

TABLE 5.4. Population Growth, 1980–2003

	Population average annual growth	
	1980–1990	1990–2003
World	1.7	1.4
Low income	2.3	2.0
Middle income	1.7	1.1
Lower middle income	1.6	1.1
Upper middle income	1.8	1.3
Low and middle income	1.0	1.5
East Asia and Pacific	1.6	1.2
Europe and Central Asia	0.9	0.1
Latin Am. and Caribbean	2.0	1.6
Mid. East and North Africa	3.1	2.1
South Asia	2.2	1.8
Sub-Saharan Africa	2.9	2.5
High Income	0.6	0.7

Source: World Bank (2005), World Development Report, p. 257; (2000/2001), pp. 278–279.

TABLE 5.5. Share of Population Living Below the Poverty Line, 1990–2001

	$1.08 a day		$2.15 a day	
	1990	2001	1990	2001
East Asia	30	15	70	47
South Asia	41	31	86	77
Latin Am. and Caribbean	11	10	28	25
North Africa and Middle East	2	2	21	23
Eastern Europe and Central Asia	1	4	5	20
Sub-Saharan Africa	45	46	75	77

Source: United Nations (2005), UN Millennium Project, p. 16.

To make things worse, between 1990 and 2002, the external debt of every low-income and middle-income region of the world increased significantly, even above the rates of economic growth in the case of middle-income countries. Annual GDP growth between 1990 and 2000 was 4.7% in low-income countries and the average annual increase of external debt between 1990 and 2002 was 2.07%. In middle-income countries, average annual GDP growth between 1990 and 2000 was 3.3%, but the average annual growth of the external debt was 5.01% (table 5.6). This shows that the debt alleviation mechanisms implemented to help the poorest countries of the world since 1990 have passed the burden from the low-income countries to the middle-income countries. This can have very negative consequences for the ability of middle-income countries to reduce poverty rates within the timeframe provided by the UN Millennium Project, especially Eastern Europe, Central Asia, Latin America and the Caribbean.

TABLE 5.6. External Debt, 1990-2002

	External debt (millions $)		
	1990	1998	2002
World			
Low income	418,922	579,545	523,464
Middle income	1,041,421	1,956,501	1,815,384
Low Middle income	-	-	1,147,339
Upper Middle income	-	-	668,045
Low and middle income	1,460,343	2,536,046	2,338,848
East Asia and Pacific	274,071	667,522	497,354
Europe and Central Asia	220,428	480,539	545,842
Latin Am. and Caribbean	475,867	786,019	727,944
Arab states	183,205	208,059	189,010
South Asia	129,899	163,775	168,349
Sub-Saharan Africa	176,873	230,132	210,350
High Income	-	-	-

Source: World Bank (2005), World Development Report, p. 257; (2000/2001), pp. 278-279.

It will be very important for the success of the project to empower the representatives of the low-income and middle-income countries in the international forums in which international economic decisions are made. Joseph E. Stiglitz raised this concern in his book *Globalization and Its Discontents*, where he argued that the International Monetary Fund (IMF) has consistently pushed a neoliberal economic model based on the so-called "Washington Consensus"[15] across the world, disregarding that on many occasions this model hurt the economies of certain countries that followed alternative models. Stiglitz also denounced that the IMF has fallen in the hands of the financial community and large US corporations, who use the IMF to advance their goals, even at the expense of fair international competition.[16]

Environmental Protection

> We must spare no effort to free all of humanity, and above all our children and grandchildren, from the threat of living on a planet irredeemably spoilt by human activities, and whose resources would no longer be sufficient for their needs.[17]

The *United Nations Millennium Report* fails the environmental test. It mainly addresses the environment to recommend a shift away from natural resource-based foreign direct investment (FDI). The report argues that resource-based FDI, such as that for oil and natural gas, does not necessarily contribute to good governance because it may result in corruption and bribes rather than development: "natural resource curse." The firms operating in natural resources may operate in the worst conditions, even war zones, and pay bribes to gain concessions over resource deposits. Therefore, the report recommends increasing transparency in bidding concessions and in the use of resulting revenue, the use of oil and gas for the development of the domestic energy infrastructure, and a plan of public investment to facilitate broad-based development.[18]

However, the project does not address the potential adverse consequences of its development recommendations on the environment. It relies on the "environmental Kuznets curve" (EKC). The EKC shows that economic growth harms the environment in the short run because of inefficiencies, inappropriate policies, insufficient funds, weak state capacity, and low political and social will. However, in the long run, environmental conditions will improve when per capita income reaches a high enough level. Slow growth reinforces the vicious cycle between poverty and environmental degradation.[19] This approach ignores that pollution does not necessarily disappear with economic development. It may just shift from one country to the next. It also ignores that an emphasis on the market may lead to the dispossession of land from the peasants by large corporations in developing countries, substituting traditional agricultural practices that were sustainable.

Examples of this were the Polonoroeste and Narmada Valley projects in Brazil and India, in the 1980s. The World Bank became the target of the fury of grassroots and environmental groups because of its policy of funding large infrastructure projects, such as these. In the state of Rondônia, the government of Brazil gave colonists plots of land to settle in this Amazonian region. The forest was cleared to build roads and farms for the settlers. The soil was not rich enough for agriculture or for cattle ranching. As a result, the settlers faced social hardship and the native population was decimated by the diseases brought in by the colonists. Between 1978 and 1991, the deforestation of the state of Rondônia grew from 1.7% to 16.1%. In the Narmada Valley of India, the government planned to build a series of dams for agriculture, but it needed to displace thousands of people who opposed this project.[20]

In the 1980s the World Bank also began to support structural adjustment programs in the countries that receive its loans. One of the goals of these reforms was to promote pro-market reforms and export-led growth, by devaluing the local currencies and to make local products cheaper in international markets. Critics argued that these reforms promote the export of natural resources, such as timber, and pollution-intensive foreign investment. Export-oriented agriculture also led local plantation owners and farmers to buy larger plots of lands for their crops, dispossessing peasants and indigenous communities of their land. The result was a decrease in food production and an increase in export-oriented crops.[21] Between 1990 and 2000, the world's average annual rate of deforestation was -0.2%. However, while in Europe the forest cover increased by 0.1%, in some developing countries the rate fell dramatically by -9.0% in Burundi, -4.3% in Comoros, -5.7% in Haiti, -4.9% in Saint Lucia, -3.9% in Rwanda, and -3.7% in Niger (see table 5.7).[22]

TABLE 5.7 Forest Cover Change, 1990–2000

Europe	0.1
Asia	-0.1
North and Central America	-0.1
Oceania	-0.2
South America	-0.4
Africa	-0.8
Niger	-3.7
Rwanda	-3.9
Saint Lucia	-4.9
Comoros	-4.3
Haiti	-5.7
Burundi	-9.0

Source: FAO, The State of the World's Forests 2003.

The creation of the Global Environment Facility (GEF) in 1991 sought to address some of these problems. Run by the World Bank, the United Nations Development Program (UNDP), and the United Nations Environment Program (UNEP), it was meant to become a "green fund" to help developing countries finance the "incremental costs" of adopting the policies for sustainable development agreed upon at the Rio Earth Summit in 1992, included in "Agenda 21." Although initially the World Bank was given a lot of power to influence the agenda, a reform in 1994 gave the GEF a new governance structure that brought together eighteen recipient-country governments, fourteen donor-country participants and five non-governmental organizations (NGOs). This reform gave developing countries more power to shape the policies of this important environmental fund. The growing amount of funds channeled to the developing countries via overseas development aid (ODA), export credit agencies and private finance mechanisms gives the institutions disbursing these funds great power to influence the activities they fund. For this reason, they should also undergo the same environmental scrutiny as the GEF and the World Bank, to make sure that governments and civil society can provide their input and help shape these projects in a way that respects the environment.[23]

Human Rights, Democracy and Good Governance

> We will spare no effort to promote democracy and strengthen the rule of law, as well as respect for all internationally recognized human rights and fundamental freedoms, including the right to development.[24]

One of the most positive changes in the world in the last twenty-five years was the gradual spread of democracy. While in 1974 only 27% of the world's countries were considered free democratic systems, in 2004 the share grew to 46%. The growth has been steady. The percentage of electoral democracies rose from around 40% in the 1980s to 61–62% between 1995 and 2004. However, in more than half of the countries of the world the political systems are only partly democratic at best, as indicated in tables 5.8 and 5.9. These statistics also conceal the fact that among the not free countries and the partly free countries there are some of the most populated countries of the world. As a result, the share of the world's population that lives in free countries is lower than that indicated by these tables. This problem is particularly acute in North Africa and the Middle East, where two thirds of the countries are not free, and in Sub-Saharan Africa, where only 23% of the countries are free.[25] One of the biggest challenges of the twenty-first century for the free societies is to engage not-free countries in a dialogue to facilitate their transition towards freer political systems. The United Nations can be an ideal body for the exchange of ideas and for engaging every country of the world.

TABLE 5.8. Democracy in the World

Region	Free	Partly free	Not free
Americas	24 (68%)	9 (26%)	2 (6%)
Asia Pacific	17 (44%)	11 (28%)	11(28%)
Central and Eastern Europe/ Former Soviet Union	12 (44%)	7 (26%)	8 (30%)
Northern Africa and Middle East	1 (6%)	5 (28%)	1 (66%)
Sub-Saharan Africa	11 (23%)	21 (44%)	16 (33%)
Western Europe	26 (96%)	1 (4%)	0 (0%)

TABLE 5.9. In Parentheses, Percent of Countries

Year	Free countries	Partly free countries	Not free countries
1974	41 (27%)	48 (32%)	63 (41%)
1984	53 (32%)	59 (35%)	55 (33%)
1994	76 (40%)	61 (32%)	54 (28%)
2004	89 (46%)	54 (28%)	49 (26%)

Source: Freedom House's Annual Global Survey of Political Rights and Liberties.

Another big challenge for democracy is corruption. Several scholars have shown that citizens in countries with higher levels of corruption express more negative evaluations of the performance of the political system and exhibit lower levels of trust in the civil servants.[26] Transparency International's "Corruption Perception Index" is consistent with these findings. Interestingly, the countries that do well in the corruption index also tend to be the ones with the highest standard of living. The index is a poll of polls, reflecting the perceptions of business people and country analysts, both resident and nonresident. Countries with a score of 9 or higher (1 being the most corrupt and 10 the lowest level of perceived corruption) are predominantly rich countries, namely Finland, New Zealand, Denmark, Iceland, Singapore, Sweden and Switzerland. The only non-Western European and non–North American countries that appear in the index with a score of 5 points or higher are (the number in parentheses indicates the position in the ranking) Singapore, 9.3 (5), Hong Kong, 8 (16), Chile, 7.4 (20), Barbados, 7.3 (21), Japan, 6.9 (24), Israel, 6.4 (26), Uruguay, 6.2 (28), Oman and United Arab Emirates, 6.1 (29), Botswana, Estonia, Slovenia, 6.0 (31), Bahrain, 5.8 (34), Taiwan, 5.6 (35), Jordan, 5.3 (37), Qatar, 5.2 (38), Malaysia and Tunisia, 5.0 (39).[27] This evidence suggests that the promotion of democracy should be coupled with the fight against corruption. The United Nations took a positive step in this direction in 2003, when the General Assembly adopted the UN Convention against Corruption.[28]

The contributors to a study published by the World Bank in 2003 argued that freedom of the press was not only an important guarantor of freedom of speech and expression, it also promotes democracy and economic development by supporting or opposing those who govern, by signaling the views and/or failures of industry, and by providing or not a voice for the people and by spreading economic information. The media can promote better economic performance when they are independent, when they provide good quality information and when they have a broad readership.[29]

Table 5.10 shows the number of journalists killed between 2002 and 2004 more than doubled. The Iraqi war was by far the single cause of death in the journalistic profession since the episode of political violence that swept Algeria in 1995, resulting in the death of fifty journalists. With the exception of Iraq, the Philippines and Colombia have the worst record. In the Philippines, those responsible for the death of journalists are local politicians and police leaders who try to silence journalists who accuse them of corruption. In Colombia, local politicians, paramilitaries of the right and communist guerrillas are responsible for the deaths.

Over 100 journalists on average were in prison every day around the world. In 2003 alone, 766 journalists were detained and at least 1,460 were physically attacked or threatened. As of December 31st, the number of journalists in prison fell from 121 in 2002 to 107 in 2004. However, the use of imprisonment to silence critical journalists has been a significant practice in some countries of Asia and the Middle East, mainly in Iran, China, Bangladesh and Cuba (see table 5.10), but also in Burma, Cameroon, Gabon, Guinea, Equatorial Guinea, North Korea, Rwanda, Togo and Zimbabwe. Judicial harassment has been common in Azerbaijan (with more than 100 physical attacks on journalists in 2004), Turkey, Turkmenistan, and Uzbekistan. Censorship is also a major method to silence critical voices. Four hundred media outlets were censored in 2002 and 501 in 2003. Even in Western Europe and North America there were reasons for concern.

TABLE 5.10. Journalists Killed and Imprisoned, 2002–2004

Year	Killed	Worst record	Imprisoned[30]	Worst record
2002	25	Colombia, 3; Philippines, 3	121	Bangladesh, 25
2003	42	Philippines, 7; Colombia, 5; Iraq, 5	120	Iran, 40
2004	53	Iraq, 19	107	China, 26; Cuba, 22

Source: Reporters sans Frontières, annual reports, 2002–2005.

In the United States several journalists faced the threat of imprisonment or house arrest for refusing to reveal their sources to judges, and in France, the homes and offices of some journalists were raided and new legislation created new press offenses punishable with imprisonment.[31]

Protecting the Vulnerable

> We will spare no effort to ensure that children and all civilian populations that suffer disproportionately the consequences of natural disasters, genocide, armed conflicts and other humanitarian emergencies are given every assistance and protection so that they can resume normal life as soon as possible.[32]

Tables 5.3 through 5.10 showed some of the most pressing issues that the "United Nations Millennium Project" needs to address. Tables 5.11, 5.12, and 5.13 provide additional social indicators that highlight the most vulnerable sectors of society. One third of the population of Africa and almost one quarter of the population of Southern Asia and Oceania are undernourished. Infant and maternal mortality is still very high, especially in Africa. Only less than half of the population of East and Southern Asia and Sub-Saharan Africa have access to improved sanitation and only half of the population of Sub-Saharan Africa and Oceania have access to improved water supply. Almost three quarters of Africans living in cities reside in slums, 59% in Southern Asia, and more than a third of those in East Asia, Western Asia and Latin America and the Caribbean. These conditions make these population sectors very vulnerable to disease.

Lack of access to education prevents poor people from escaping these living conditions. Among the poor, women are particularly vulnerable because they do not yet have equal access to basic education, especially in Africa, where 22 million girls do not receive primary education. The ratio of women attending secondary education is still much lower than that of males in Africa, Asia and Oceania. Access to telephone services in Southeast and Southern Asia, Africa and Oceania is a privilege that only less than 20% of the population enjoy. Some of the major causes of death in the twentieth century have affected the population at risk in these areas more than any other sector. Half a billion people were killed by smallpox in the world, 71 million by smoking,[33] 11,700,000 by AIDS between 1981 and 1998 alone, 8.5 million were murdered, and 3.5 million were killed by natural disasters.[34] A successful development strategy must empower these vulnerable population groups so they can protect themselves.

TABLE 5.11. Social Statistics

	Undernourishment prevalence (%)		Net enrolled in primary education (%)		Ratio of girls to boys in secondary education		Share of urban population living in slums	
	1990	2001	1990	2001	1990	2001	1990	2001
East Asia	16	11	98	92	-	-	41	36
SE Asia	17	13	92	91	0.97	0.98	37	28
South Asia	25	22	73	80	0.74	0.77	64	59
West Asia	7	10	81	83	0.76	0.79	34	35
North Africa	5	4	82	92	0.94	0.96	38	28
Sub-Saharan Africa	35	33	54	62	0.81	0.79	72	72
Latin Am. and Caribbean	13	10	86	96	1.09	1.07	35	32
Oceania	25	27	74	79	0.89	0.93	25	24

TABLE 5.12. Social Statistics

	Telephone lines and cellular subscribers (per 100 population)	
	1990	2001
East Asia	2	38
Southeastern Asia	1	16
Southern Asia	1	5
Western Asia	10	42
Northern Africa	3	17
Sub-Saharan Africa	1	5
Latin Am. and Caribbean	6	36
Oceania	3	9

Source: United Nations (2005), UN Millennium Project, 18–19.

TABLE 5.13. Social Statistics

	Under-five mortality rate (per 1,000)		Maternal mortality (per 100,000 live births)		Access to improved water supply (%)		Access to improved sanitation (%)	
	1990	2001	1990	2001	1990	2001	1990	2001
East Asia	48	38	-	55	72	78	24	45
SE Asia	78	48	-	210	73	79	48	61
S. Asia	126	93	-	520	71	84	20	37
W. Asia	68	61	-	190	83	88	79	79
N. Africa	87	41	-	130	88	90	65	73
Sub-Saharan Africa	186	174	-	920	49	58	32	36
Latin Am. and Caribbean	54	34	-	190	83	89	69	75
Oceania	86	78	-	240	51	52	58	55

Source: United Nations (2005), UN Millennium Project, pp. 18–19.

Meeting the Special Needs of Africa

> We will support the consolidation of democracy in Africa and assist Africans in their struggle for lasting peace, poverty eradication and sustainable development, thereby bringing Africa into the mainstream of the world economy.[35]

The previous tables show that the Sub-Saharan African population has the largest number of people in the risk sectors. Thirty-three percent of Sub-Saharan Africans were undernourished, only 62% had access to primary education (22 million girls did not receive primary education), 70% of those living in cities lived in slums, only 58% Sub-Saharan Africans had access to improved water supply and 36% had access to improved sanitation, and only 5% had access to telephone services. Infant mortality was 179/100,000 and maternal mortality 920/100,000. Africa had the worst rate of deforestation in the 1990s (-0.8% annually). Only 23% of African countries were free democracies in 2005. And yet, the ability of Sub-Saharan African societies to address these problems was severely constrained by its growing external debt. Sub-Saharan Africa's external debt grew by 1.57% annually between 1990 and 2002, while annual GDP growth per capita between 1990 and 2001 fell by 0.1% annually, and political violence plagued several African societies in the 1990s, claiming the lives of 2,200,000 in Rwanda, Angola, Somalia, Liberia, and Burundi alone. These economic and political conditions make it impossible for Africa to achieve the social and economic goals stated in the *UN Millennium Report* unless serious efforts are developed to tackle these challenges.

Reaffirmation of Faith in the Values and Principles of the UN Charter and Strengthening the United Nations

> We will spare no effort to make the United Nations a more effective instrument for pursuing all of these priorities: the fight for development for all the peoples of the world, the fight against poverty, ignorance and disease; the fight against injustice; the fight against violence, terror and crime; and the fight against the degradation and destruction of our common home.[36]

The US system is an imperfect institutional body. It faces great challenges to address the pressing issues discussed in this chapter. It lacks the resources to undertake the large projects needed to improve living standards in the poor regions. It also lacks the political clout to bring world leaders together and it has disappointed many because it is expected to act in spheres beyond its competencies. However, over the years it has become the main international deliberative and decision-making body of the international community. It legitimizes collective security operations and some of its agencies have become the world leading actors in the fight against poverty, political oppression, and cultural and environmental protection, among other issues.

Point VIII.30 of the UN Millennium Declaration calls for a reform of the UN framework to increase its effectiveness. It reaffirms the central position of the General Assembly as the chief deliberative, policymaking, and representative organ of the United Nations. It calls for reform of the Security Council, strengthening the Economic and Social Council and the International Court of Justice, and closer and more frequent consultations and coordination among the bodies of the UN to achieve a fully coordinated approach to peace and development, including the IMF, the World Bank ("the Bretton Woods institutions") and the WTO. It also recommends giving greater opportunities to the private sector, NGOs and civil society to contribute to the realization of the goals of the United Nations.[37]

The UN Millennium Declaration and the *UN Millennium Report* provide a great opportunity to address the challenges discussed in this chapter. The commitment of the heads of government that signed the declaration serves as a manifestation of their good faith. However, conditions in Africa, the Middle East, Eastern Europe and Central Asia worsened between 1990 and 2005 and progress in Latin America and the Caribbean was negligible. To be successful in reversing these trends the UN system faces a major problem of lack of political will. Unless its main contributors accept to commit more resources and political energy, the declaration and the report will become another missed opportunity.

Notes

1. "United Nations Millennium Declaration," UN resolution 55/2, eighth plenary meeting, September 8, 2000.
2. United Nations (2005), UN Millennium Project, New York, p. 1.
3. F. D. Roosevelt's "Four Freedoms" speech to the Congress of the United States, January 6, 1941.
4. "United Nations Millennium Declaration," II.8.
5. Mary Ellen O'Connell, *International Law and the Use of Force*, New York: Foundation Press, 2005.
6. Zbigniew Brzezinski, *Out of Control: Global Turmoil on the Eve of the Twenty-first Century*, New York: Maxwell Macmillan International, 1993.
7. Murray, C. J. L., King, G., López, A. D., Tomijima, N., and Grug, E. G., "Armed Conflict as a Public Health Problem," *BMH*, 321 (February 2002), pp. 346–349.
8. Kenneth Waltz, "The Spread of Nuclear Weapons: More May Be Better," Adelphi Papers, Oxford University Press, vol. 17 (1981), pp. 1–29.
9. Robert O. Keohane and Joseph S. Nye, *Power and Interdependence* (3rd ed.), New York: Longman, 2001.

10. A detailed analysis of the sources of conflict is beyond the scope of this article. See Seyom Brown, *The Causes and Prevention of War* (2nd ed.), New York: St. Martin's Press, 1994; and Richard K. Betts, *Conflict after the Cold War. Arguments on Causes of War and Peace*, New York: Longman Publishers, 2002.
11. United Nations, "Charter of the United Nations."
12. Stephen M. Walt, "Beyond bin Laden: Reshaping U.S. Foreign Policy," *International Security* 26(3), (2001–2002 Winter), pp. 56–78.
13. "United Nations Millennium Declaration," III.11.
14. United Nations (2005), UN Millennium Project, New York, pp. 28–29.
15. John Williamson, *Latin American Adjustment. How Much Has Happened?*, Institute for International Economics, Washington, DC, 1990.
16. Joseph E. Stiglitz, *Globalization and Its Discontents*, New York: W. W. Norton, 2002.
17. "United Nations Millennium Declaration," IV-21.
18. United Nations (2005), UN Millennium Project, p. 48.
19. Jennifer Clapp and Peter Dauvergne, *Paths to a Green World. The Political Economy of the Global Environment*, Cambridge: MIT Press, 2005, pp. 91–94.
20. Bruce Rich, *Mortgaging the Earth: The World Bank, Environmental Impoverishment, and the Crisis of Development*, London: Earthscan, 1994, pp. 152–153; Uday Turaga, "Damming Waters and Wisdom: Protest in the Narmada River Valley," *Technology in Society* 22 (2000), pp. 237–253.
21. Clapp and Dauvergne, *Paths to a Green World*, pp. 203–207.
22. Food and Agriculture Organization (FAO), *The State of the World's Forests 2003*.
23. Clapp and Dauvergne, *Paths to a Green World*, pp. 207–216.
24. "United Nations Millennium Declaration," V.24.
25. Freedom House's Annual Global Survey of Political Rights and Liberties.
26. Christopher J. Anderson and Yuliya V. Tverdova, "Corruption, Political Allegiances and Attitudes toward Government in Contemporary Democracies," *American Journal of Political Science* 47(1) (January 2003), pp. 91–109; Walter Little and Eduardo Posada-Carbó, eds., *Political Corruption in Europe and Latin America*, New York: St. Martin's Press, 1996.
27. Transparency International Corruption Perception Index 2004 draws on eighteen surveys provided to Transparency International between 2002 and 2004, conducted by twelve independent institutions. Source: Transparency International (2004), "Corruption is rampant in 60 countries, and the public sector is plagued by bribery, says TI. Transparency International's Corruption Perception Index 2004 ranks a record 146 countries; most oil-producing nations are prone to high corruption," released in London, October 20, 2004.
28. "Adoption of UN Convention against Corruption," *The American Journal of International Law* 98(1) (January 2004), pp. 182–184.
29. Roumeen Islam, " Into the Looking Glass: What the Media Tell and Why: An Overview," *The Right To Tell: The Role of Mass Media in Economic Development*, Washington, DC: World Bank, 2003, p. 1.
30. As of December 31st each year.
31. Reporters sans Frontières, annual reports 2003–2005.
32. "United Nations Millennium Declaration," VI.26.

33. This figure refers only to the United States, Europe, countries of the former USSR, Canada, Japan, Australia and New Zealand.
34. Mannfred Hollinger, *Introduction to Pharmacology*, Taylor & Francis, Washington, DC, 2002; Peto, R., Lopez, A.D., Boreham, J., Thun, M., and Heath C. Jr., "Mortality from Tobacco in Developed Countries: Indirect Estimation from National Vital Statistics," *Lancet* 339(8804) (1992), pp. 1268–1278; Munich Re Insurance, Twentieth Century Atlas, Death tolls, http://www.munichre.com; Joint United Nations Programme on HIV/AIDS, http://www.unaids.org/highband/document/epidemio/june98/index.html; Twentieth Century Atlas, Death tolls. Retrived, December 6, 2005.
35. "United Nations Millennium Declaration," VII.27.
36. Ibid., VIII.29.
37. Ibid., VIII.30.

6

Freedom, Fear, and Terrorism in Democratic Societies

LOUIS A. PAGLIARO AND ANN MARIE PAGLIARO

> In this possibly terminal phase of human existence, democracy and freedom are more than just ideals to be valued—they may be essential to survival.
> NOAM AVRAM CHOMSKY (1928–)

The purpose of this chapter is to consider the notions of freedom, fear, and terrorism and their relationship in the context of democratic societies.[1] The chapter reflects our underlying personal belief that a constitutional democracy is the preferred form of government for everyone—everywhere. We believe, too, that people have an inherent desire to be free. However, we appreciate that freedom is neither free of cost nor certain of outcome. At this time in history, terrorists, worldwide, are increasingly attempting to subvert democracy and its attendant freedoms through acts of terrorism aimed at instilling fear and eliciting cowardice among free people and those who are working to build democratic societies. We argue that, ultimately, courage to fight terrorism is requisite for the preservation and globalization of democracy, whereas cowardice—retreat and appeasement—will result in its loss as well as the loss of its attendant freedoms (figure 6.1).[2]

In order to delineate our argument clearly and parsimoniously and to avoid, or at least earnestly attempt to minimize possible resultant semantic debate and spurious rebuttal of our colloquy, we begin with some basic definitions and our assumptions.

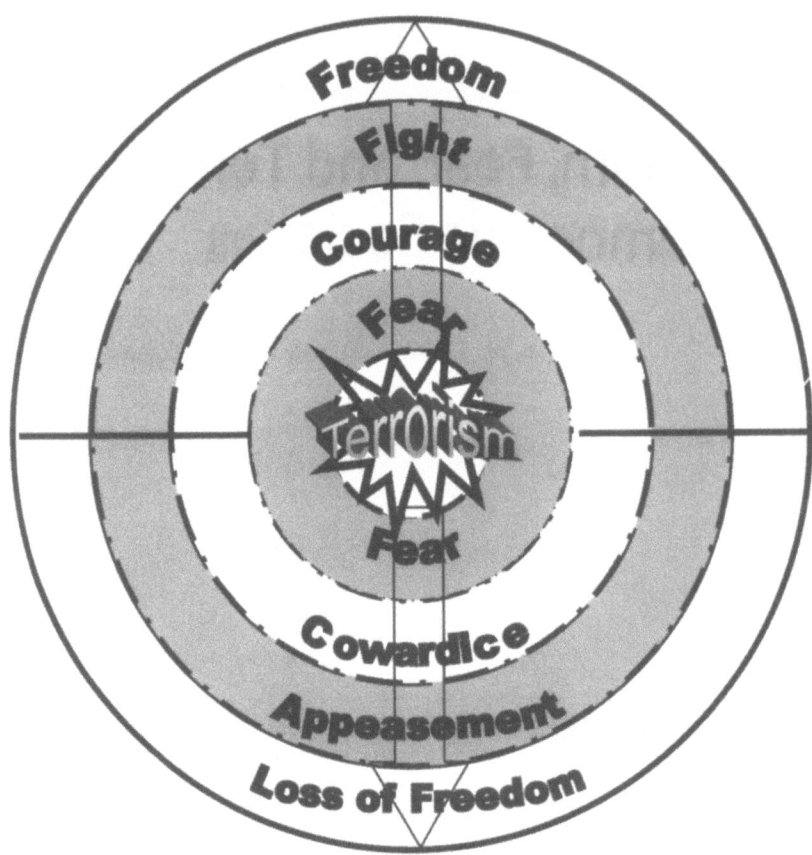

FIGURE 6.1. The Relationship of Terrorism to Fear and Freedom.

Definitions[3]

Several words, in common usage today, are inherent to our argument and require definition. These words include: *freedom, fear, terror,* and *terrorism*. Each of these words are defined and initially briefly considered in regard to our argument.

Freedom

> Knock off the chains of heart-debasing slavery; give to man, of every color and of every clime, Freedom, which stamps him image of his God.
> JAMES GRAINGER (1721–1766).[4]

Freedom is defined as *the power or right for a person to act, speak, or think without restriction or interference from others.*[5] In a democracy, freedom is indigenous and ubiquitous,[6] but generally restricted in order to ensure that individual and minority rights are protected without the loss of majority rights or the will of the people.[7] Thus, for example, under the guise of freedom of speech, falsely yelling "fire" in a movie theater is not permitted nor is jokingly declaring that one's briefcase contains a bomb while standing in line to board an international flight.

Fear

> No passion so effectively robs the mind of all its powers of acting and reasoning as fear.
> JOHN BERRYMAN (1729–1797).[8]

Fear is defined as an unpleasant emotion caused by the threatened anticipation of danger, pain, or harm.[9] Thus, children may fear the dark, an injection at the doctor's office, or a visit to the dentist. An adolescent may fear going to school where he or she may be attacked, robbed, or otherwise abused by a bully or violent gang member. A young soldier may fear driving down a road that had previously been booby-trapped with roadside explosive devices, a young woman may fear the birth of her first child, and an elderly man may fear being admitted to a residential nursing home.[10]

Fear arises as a normal and automatic response to a recognized threat, real or perceived. It may result in a variety of unpleasant feelings including feelings of uneasiness or dread and an urge to escape. As a normal emotion, fear can lead to rapid self-protective action (e.g., physically defending oneself or removing oneself from the threatening situation). [11,12] Fear is counteracted by conscious, voluntary acts of courage. These acts are many and varied. For example, they include making a military bombing flight to Iran to destroy nuclear reactors with the knowledge that a safe return is highly unlikely. They include casting a vote when the ink on one's finger may bring death to both oneself and one's family. They include using the subway or other public transportation to get to work despite terrorist warnings. And they include attending a wedding reception at a popular resort or just going out to eat in a favorite restaurant in an area where terrorist activity has previously occurred.

Terror

> There is no terror in a bang, only in the anticipation of it.
> ALFRED HITCHCOCK (1899–1980).

Terror is defined as *extreme or intense fear that can be overpowering*. The instillation of terror among free people is the fervent desire of terrorists as they strive toward their goal of ideological, political, or religious domination.

Terrorism

> The spirit of democracy cannot be established in the midst of terrorism, whether governmental or popular.
>
> MOHANDAS K. [MAHATMA] GANDHI (1869–1948).

Terrorism is defined as *the generation of fear among civilians by means of the calculated use of violence, or the threat of violence*.[13] Terrorism is used as a tactic by terrorists[14] in their attempt to attain their goals, which are most often ideological, political, or religious in nature.[15] Terrorists achieve their intended goals only if the target group or society becomes so imbued with fear that, feeling helpless, it consequently resorts to appeasement or retreat (also see related discussion on Terror and Appeasement below) as a generally futile means of self-defense or self-preservation.[16]

Assumptions

The development and advancement of our argument are predicated on the following assumptions:

1. That the premise proposed by G. W. Hegel (1770–1831): that *wherever there is law there is freedom*, is rejected. This premise is unduly simplistic and patently false. For example, there were many laws in Nazi Germany, but relatively few freedoms, particularly if one was Jewish, homosexual, or otherwise politically or socially marginalized.
2. That the premise proposed by Jean Jacques Rousseau (1712–1778): that the collective will of the legislative group of a community is always right and, consequently, that individuals who refuse to obey the *general will* should be forced to do so, is rejected. This premise *means nothing less than that they will be forced to be free* [17] and, thus, is incommensurable with our definition of *freedom*.[18] By corollary, we also reject the notion that laws are always right and just. Indeed, there are times and circumstances where a person can only obtain freedom, not by following the established law, but by deliberately breaking it—consider, for example, the related experiences of Mohandas K. (Mahatma) Gandhi (1869–1948) and Martin Luther King (1929–1968) during the last century. These two men urged their followers to break the law—not with violent terrorist acts, but with peaceful, nonviolent resistance.[19] Both were ultimately successful in garnishing significant additional freedom for their followers.
3. That John Dewey's (1859–1952) premise: that *warranted assertability* can be used as a substitute for truth when, as a result, the effect or outcome is

more desirable, is rejected. So, too, is the closely related philosophical assertion that *the end justifies the means*. Although these notions[20] are commonly embraced and possess verisimilitude, they are, in fact, devoid of philosophical veracity and lack objective moral grounding (we reject a teleological view of morality). Upon individual analysis, these notions most often are found to be adopted by their proponents simply as a rationalization for abhorrent and otherwise unjustifiable behaviors (e.g., the genocide of Jews during World War II or, more recently, the genocide of the bushmen in Botswana and the Tutsi minority in Rwanda).

4. We cite the clichéd and hackneyed adage *one man's terrorist is another man's freedom fighter*[21] as a contextual example of warranted assertability and, as such, this adage is totally repudiated. Simply put, *a terrorist is a terrorist*, regardless of age, color, ethnic origin, gender, nationality, political persuasion, race, or religion. The end does not justify the means nor does it change the character or essence of terrorist behavior (which also cannot be assuaged by any amount of political demagoguery).[22] (Also see Assumption #3 for related discussion)

5. That a democratic form of government (i.e., a constitutional democracy), although imperfect, is preferred to other available forms of government—such as dictatorships, monarchies, oligarchies, or theocracies—because democracies offer the greatest opportunity for freedom for the masses of its citizenry and not, as in other forms of government, primarily for its dictator, aristocracy, ruling class, or religious leaders.

As noted by Winston Churchill (1874–1965):[23]

No one pretends that democracy is perfect or all-wise. Indeed, it has been said that democracy is the worst form of Government except all those other forms that have been tried from time to time.

The Globalization of Democracy

We begin with the words of Franklin Delano Roosevelt (1882–1945):

We look forward to a world founded upon four essential human freedoms. The first is freedom of speech and expression—everywhere in the world. The second is freedom of every person to worship God in his own way—everywhere in the world. The third is freedom from want—everywhere in the world. The fourth is freedom from fear . . . anywhere in the world.[24]

Roosevelt spoke literally to a global perspective on freedom and fear because he recognized, as did others of his time, before his time, and since his time, that one's own individual freedom is inextricably enmeshed in the freedom of others. For example, in 1912, Clarence Seward Darrow (1857–1938) noted that "You can only protect your liberties in this world by protecting the other man's freedom. You can only be free if I am free."[25] Three decades later, Wendell Lewis Willkie (1892–1944) noted that:

"Freedom is an indivisible word. If we want to enjoy it, and fight for it, we must be prepared to extend it to everyone, whether they are rich or poor, whether they agree with us or not, no matter what their race or the color of their skin."[26] Two decades later, Christopher Hill (1912–2003) noted that "Only very slowly and late have men come to realize that unless freedom is universal it is only extended privilege."[27]

Another four decades later, in response to terrorist actions and growing terrorist threats against the United States of America and other democratic countries, President George W. Bush reasserted the related American strategy:

> Three and a half years ago, the United States mourned our dead, gathered our resolve, and accepted a mission. We made a decision to stop threats to the American people before they arrive on our shores, and we have acted on that decision. We're also determined to seek and support the growth of democratic movements and institutions in every nation and culture, with the ultimate goal of ending tyranny in our world.
>
> This objective will not be achieved easily, or all at once, or primarily by force of arms. We know that freedom, by definition, must be chosen and that the democratic institutions of other nations will not look like our own. Yet we also know that our security increasingly depends on the hope and progress of other nations now simmering in despair and resentment. And that hope and progress are found only in the advance of freedom.
>
> This advance is a consistent theme of the American strategy—from the Fourteen Points, to the Four Freedoms, to the Marshall Plan, to the Reagan Doctrine. Yet the success of this approach does not depend on grand strategy alone. We are confident that the desire for freedom, even when repressed for generations, is present in every human heart. And that desire can emerge with sudden power to change the course of history. ... The trumpet of freedom has been sounded, and that trumpet never calls retreat.[28]

The Relationship between Fear and Freedom

Baruch Spinoza (1632–1677) was one of the first Western philosophers to speak to the relationship between the tyranny of fear and the need for it to be suppressed or abolished in order for liberty and freedom to flourish:

> A free man thinks of nothing less than of death; and his wisdom is a meditation not of death, but of life.[29]

Thus, to follow Spinoza's philosophy and to be truly *free*, people must be able to liberate themselves from the fear of physical harm and death that have become the hallmark and currency of terrorists. Free people, in order to remain free, must have courage and be able to embolden themselves with life and the daily events of living—as the people of London did during World War II bombings of their city and as they have done during the more recent bombings of their transit system; as the people of Israel have done for several generations against terrorist suicide bombers; and as the people of New York and Washington, DC, have done since the terrorist attacks of September 11, 2001.[30]

Since the very founding of their democratic society in 1776, the American people recognized and demonstrated that freedom is neither assured nor without cost to its citizens. Freedom must be defended by the courage and determination of free people—courage and determination that also may require self-sacrifice:

The progress of liberty is a powerful trend. Yet, we also know that liberty, if not defended, can be lost. The success of freedom is not determined by some dialectic of history. By definition, the success of freedom rests upon the choices and the courage of free peoples, and upon their willingness to sacrifice. In the trenches of World War I, through a two-front war in the 1940s, the difficult battles of Korea and Vietnam, and in missions of rescue and liberation on nearly every continent, Americans have amply displayed our willingness to sacrifice for liberty.[31]

A particularly germane and poignant example of Americans, who, when confronted with a horrendous terrorist act, responded not with trepidation and offers of appeasement—generated by fear—but, rather, with courage, which was summoned to liberate themselves from the fear of physical harm and sure death as they made the ultimate sacrifice to preserve the life, liberty, and pursuit of happiness for others—their fellow Americans—this is the story of the passengers on United Airlines flight #93 on September 11, 2001.

Terror and Appeasement

Appeasement can be simply defined as attempting to placate someone, such as a school yard bully or terrorist, by agreeing to his or her demands in the hope that by doing so, the bully or terrorist will not follow through with his or her threats. Thus, the school-aged child, who has already had an eye blackened by a bully for not giving him his lunch money, may, as an act of appeasement—in a generally fruitless attempt to avoid future beatings—give the bully his lunch money for the rest of the school year while promising not to tell anyone.[32] Likewise, the people of a democratic society, having experienced the bombing of their cities and the murder of their civilian populace may, as an act of appeasement, agree to give up their fight against terrorism, or abandon people of other countries in their fight against terrorism in an effort to protect themselves. Although purported motives may differ, there is no practical difference between the school yard bully and the terrorist, except that the stakes are significantly much higher in regard to the latter.

Happiness, Freedom, and Peace for All

> Happiness is the only sanction of life, where happiness fails, existence remains a mad and lamentable experiment.
> GEORGE SANTAYANA (1863–1952).[33]

A lesson recurrent in history, which all free people should pay heed to and learn from, is that to be *happy*[34] one cannot partake of a policy of appeasement—as was tried, for example, by Neville Chamberlain (1869–1940), and failed, during World War II with the Nazis.[35] Perhaps this is true, at least in part, because terrorists generally have feelings of extreme hatred toward their target group/society and, as explained by Peter Forster, *as far as we know, most terrorists feel that they are doing nothing wrong when they kill and injure people, or damage property*.[36] As noted by Thucydides (455–400 BC): "Happiness depends on being free, and freedom depends on being courageous"—on being able to confront fear and terror, particularly when this fear and terror have been caused by one's enemies.[37] Two thousand years later, Voltaire (Francois Marie Arovet, 1694–1778) expounded a related corollary:

> So long as the people do not care to exercise their freedom, those who wish to tyrannize will do so; for tyrants are active and ardent, and will devote themselves in the name of any number of gods, religious and otherwise, to put shackles upon sleeping men.

As noted in a speech by President George W. Bush over 200 years later in 2005:

> By now it should be clear that decades of excusing and accommodating tyranny, in the pursuit of stability, have only led to injustice and instability and tragedy. It should be clear that the advance of democracy leads to peace, because governments that respect the rights of their people also respect the rights of their neighbors. It should be clear that the best antidote to radicalism and terror is the tolerance and hope kindled in free societies.[38]

Summary and Conclusions

We conclude with the words of Franklin Delano Roosevelt: *The only thing we have to fear is fear itself*.[39] Truly a sentiment and philosophy shared and supported by others through the ages, including: Michel de Montaigne (1533–1592), *The thing I fear most is fear;*[40] Francis Bacon (1561–1626), *Nothing is terrible except fear itself;*[41] Arthur Wellesley, Duke of Wellington (1769–1852), *The only thing I am afraid of is fear;*[42] and Henry David Thoreau (1817–1862), *Nothing is so much to be feared as fear.*[43]

Some, particularly those who have never been in war or who have never been directly confronted by terrorism, may think that these sentiments are no more than hackneyed expressions. This simply is not so. In direct support of our contention is the often asked question, "How can I avoid fear?" The answer is that a person cannot avoid fear—fear is an *ingrained* psychological response to an aversive stimulus (discussed earlier), in our context—of a terrorist attack or threat. This is why so many great men have expressed concern over fear—because they each came to the realization that fear can neither be escaped nor avoided. Because a person cannot simply escape or avoid fear, he or she must learn to confront it so as not to be controlled by it. This is no mean feat. It takes personal courage[44] and determination.

> Courage is not simply one of the virtues but the form of every virtue at the testing point.
> C. S. Lewis (1898–1963)[45]

In order to both maintain and sustain our democratic way of life, we must, individually and collectively, confront terrorism directly and courageously until it is eradicated and democracy is flourishing around the world. To do so we must recognize that the principal tool of the terrorist is not the car or truck loaded with explosives, nor the suicide bomber with explosives strapped to his or her chest, but the *fear* and *terror* that is generated through these murderous and cowardly actions.

Knowing this, the words of Thucydides uttered over 2,000 years ago appear to offer sound and appropriate guidance for future generations of free people and those striving to be free, "For now it remains to rival what they have done and, knowing the secret of happiness to be freedom and the secret of freedom a brave heart, not idly to stand aside from the enemy's onset."[46]

Notes

1. Democratic societies are composed of free men and women. While selected reference citations may use the more traditional forms of "he" and "man" or "mankind," we interpret and use these citations inclusively. As well, our argument and conclusions apply equally to both men and women.
2. The complex and variable relationship among terrorism, fear, and freedom is illustrated. The initial universal response to terrorism is fear. Courage or cowardice then becomes the primary intervening variable. In the presence of cowardice, fear generally leads to appeasement and, ultimately, to loss of freedom. In the presence of courage, fear is met with a willingness to fight for freedom and, ultimately, its attainment or preservation.

3. Definitions were modified from the *Compact Oxford English Dictionary*, New York: Oxford University Press, 2003.
4. James Grainger (1764), *The Sugar Cane* in An Essay on the More Common West-India Diseases, 2nd Ed. (Jamaica: Alexander Aikman, 1802), 88–92.
5. In this context, *freedom*, for example, is that which Sisyphus experiences as he walks down the mountainside while the stone rolls down before him even though he knows that again, and eternally, he must roll it back up to the mountain top (Albert Camus [1913–1960], *Myth of Sisyphus [1943/1955]*).
6. This is generally accomplished by the enactment of laws by an elected legislature, their interpretation by the judiciary, and their enforcement by officers of the law.
7. Consider these related words of President George W. Bush:

   The advance of freedom is the calling of our time; it is the calling of our country. From the Fourteen Points to the Four Freedoms, to the Speech at Westminster, America has put our power at the service of principle. We believe that liberty is the design of nature; we believe that liberty is the direction of history. We believe that human fulfillment and excellence come in the responsible exercise of liberty. And we believe that freedom—the freedom we prize—is not for us alone, it is the right and the capacity of all mankind. (President Bush Discusses Freedom in Iraq and Middle East, Remarks by the President at the 20th Anniversary of the National Endowment of Democracy, United States Chamber of Commerce, Washington DC, November 6, 2003). Available: http://www.Whitehouse.Gov/news/releases/2003/11/print/20031106-2.html, accessed September 12, 2006. This is generally accomplished by the enactment of laws by an elected legislature, their interpretation by the judiciary, and their enforcement by officers of the law.

8. John Berryman (1757), *On the Sublime and Beautiful*. In E. Burke (Reprint). London: Basil Blackwell.
9. This type of fear is specific or generalized, real, and rational. It may be extreme, but it is not the irrational and unwarranted type of fear that is psychologically known as *phobia*. See n. 11.
10. Throughout this chapter, we may ascribe some characteristic trait (e.g., bravery) to a specific group of people (e.g., Americans, children); we do so with the patent recognition that the trait most likely does not apply to all members of the group.
11. This is physiologically referred to as the "fight or flight response." When a person is frightened, an increased amount of adrenaline is released in the body, thus preparing the person for "fight" or "flight."
12. Fear is often used when what is meant more precisely is *anxiety*, *panic*, or *phobia*. *Anxiety*, a vague feeling of uneasiness or apprehension, usually refers to fear of uncertain origin. Where fear is usually associated with responses to a consciously recognized external threat, anxiety is, as noted by Søren Kierkegaard (1813–1855), the full experience of fear in the absence of a known threat. *Panic*, clinically an extreme form of anxiety, is a sudden occurrence of acute intense fear often associated with frantic attempts to escape. A *phobia* is an intense, irrational fear associated with a specific object, situation, or event. A phobic response is not propor-

tional to the threat, cannot be explained or reasoned away, and leads to avoidance of the feared object, situation, or event.
13. We appreciate that there is no one universally accepted definition of terrorism and that it can be defined and classified according to several different perspectives. See, for example, the following definition proffered by the *Encyclopedia of Marxism*:

An aspect of psychological warfare whose aim is to instill fear and intimidation among both civilians and the military/police through the use of limited but concentrated violence. The basis of terrorist actions are a lack of popular support and the need to subjugate the popular will through destructive acts of violence causing widespread fear and terror (*Marxists Internet Archive, 1999–2005*).

14. Edmund Burke (1729–1797) first used the term, *terrorist*, in reference to the machinations of the Jacobins who set the policy for the French Revolution and, in particular, the formal adoption, on September 5, 1793, by the National Convention of *Terror* as the order of the day. The *regime de la terreur* prevailed in France from 1793 to 1794, principally under the leadership of the French revolutionary Maximilien Robespierre. Edmund Burke popularized the English use of the term, terrorists, with his related writings and the phrase: "Those hellhounds called terrorists."
15. We will not be addressing the causes of terrorism in this chapter. However, we appreciate that the causes are diverse and multifactorial and include specific cultural, economic, historical, political, psychological, and religious factors.
16. A contemporary example of this phenomenon was observed among the people of Spain who, subsequent to the terrorist train bombings in Madrid on March 11, 2003 (on the eve of the scheduled national political elections), defeated the ruling party that supported the war in Iraq and voted in a party that campaigned on removing Spanish troops from Iraq and ending Spanish support of the war.
17. Jean Jacques Rousseau (1762/1968), *Social Contracte*. Translated and introduced by Maurice Cranston. Harmondworth, Middlesex, England and New York: Penguin Books.
18. Indeed the phrase *forced to be free* is, from our philosophical viewpoint, patently oxymoronic.
19. "Non-violence is the first article of my faith. It is also the last article of my creed" (Mohandas K. [Mahatma] Gandhi, Speech at Shahi Bag, March 18, 1922).
20. These notions are related to the philosophies of pragmatism and utilitarianism (i.e., subjective efficacy and utility in practical application provide a standard for "truthfulness" in the case of statements, "rightness" in the case of actions, and "value" in the case of appraisals, as reflected by William James, 1842–1910).
21. The origin of this idiom is unknown, but the closely related phrase *One man's terrorist is another man's liberator* has been ascribed to Carlos Marighella. (See note 22).
22. In regard to related attempts at demagoguery, consider, for example, the words of Maximilien Robespierre (1758–1794), the leader of the twelve-man committee of Public Safety that was elected by the National Convention and essentially governed France during the height of the French Revolution:

In the spring of popular government in time of peace is virtue, the springs of popular government in revolution are at once *virtue* and *terror*. Virtue, without which terror is fatal; terror, without which virtue is powerless. Terror is nothing other than justice, prompt, severe, inflexible; it is therefore an emanation of virtue; it is not so much a special principle as it is a consequence of the general principle of democracy applied to our country's most urgent needs.

It has been said that terror is the principle of despotic government. Does your government therefore resemble despotism? Yes, as the sword that gleams in the hands of the heroes of liberty resembles that with which the henchmen of tyranny are armed. Let the despot govern by terror his brutalized subjects; he is right, as a despot. Subdue by terror the enemies of liberty, and you will be right, as founders of the Republic. The government of the revolution is liberty's despotism against tyranny. Is force made only to protect crime? And is the thunderbolt not destined to strike the heads of the proud? (*Marxism and ethics*. Available: http://www.marxists.org/reference/subject/ethics/index.htm, accessed October 9, 2006)

Or consider the words of Carlos Marighella (1930–1971), a Brazilian revolutionary leader and author of the *Minimanual of the Urban Guerrilla* (1969) from which the following was extracted:

The accusation of *violence* or *terrorism* no longer has the negative meaning it used to have. It has acquired new clothing; a new color. It does not divide, it does not discredit; on the contrary, it represents a center of attraction. Today, to be *violent* or a *terrorist* is a quality that ennobles any honorable person, because it is an act worthy of a revolutionary engaged in armed struggle against the shameful military dictatorship and its atrocities. (Available: http://www.marxists.org/archive/marighella-carlos/1969/06/minimanual-urban-guerrilla/index.htm, accessed October 9, 2006.)

23. Winston Churchill, 1947, *House of Commons Speech*, November 11.
24. Franklin Delano Roosevelt (1941), *Message to Congress*, January 6.
25. Clarence Seward Darrow (1912), *Darrow takes the Stand*. Available: http://www.nationalmediaservices.com/justice/itemdt001n.html, accessed October 9, 2006
26. Wendell Lewis Willkie (1943), *One World*. New York: The Limited Editions Club, Chapter 13.
27. Christopher Hill (1961), *Century of Revolution*. New York: W.W. Norton.
28. *President Bush Discusses Freedom in Iraq and Middle East*, Remarks by the President at the 20th Anniversary of the National Endowment of Democracy, United States Chamber of Commerce, Washington, DC, November 6, 2003). Available: http://www.Whitehouse.Gov/news/releases/2003/11/print/20031106-2.html
29. Baruch Spinoza (1677/2004), *Ethics—Of the Power of the Understanding, or of Human Freedom*. Whitefish, MT: Kessinger Publishing.
30. This concept should be particularly resonant among Americans who live in *the land of the free and the home of the brave*—as immortalized in a poem written in 1814 by Francis Scott Key (1779–1843), *The Star-Spangled Banner*—a poem that would, in 1931, become the

National Anthem of the United States of America.
31. *President Bush Discusses Freedom in Iraq and Middle East*, Remarks by the President at the 20th Anniversary of the National Endowment of Democracy, United States Chamber of Commerce, Washington, DC, November 6, 2003). Available: http: // www.whitehouse.gov/ news/releases/2003/11/ print/20031106–2.html
32. In addition to being victimized by a beating, and future threats of more, and having paid the demanded extortion, nothing has been done to guarantee that the bully will keep his or her end of the bargain—not continuing to beat the school-aged child whenever he chooses to or asking for more and more money. The bully also uses fear and intimidation to prevent other children from *coming to the aid of* or otherwise helping the "victim," for fear of becoming victims themselves.
33. George Santayana (1905/1936), *Life of Reason*. New York: C. Scribner Sons, (Vol. 1, Chapter 10).
34. Happiness, in this context, reflects what has come to be valued among free people living peaceably in a democratic society as *life, liberty, and the pursuit of happiness*.
35. *How horrible, fantastic, incredible it is that we should be digging trenches and trying on gas-masks here because of a quarrel in a far away country between people of whom we know nothing.* (Neville Chamberlain, Radio broadcast, September 27, 1938)
36. Peter M. Forster (2005, p. 4). *The Psychology of Terror—The Mind of the Terrorist* (pp. 1–15). Available: www. Blue-oceans.Com/psychology/terror_psych.Html at Blue Ocean Publisher
37. Thucydides, 455–400 BC, *The History of the Peloponnesian War, 431–413 BC*. Whitefish, MT: Kessinger.
38. *President discusses war on terror*, National Defense University, Fort Lesley J. McNair, March 8, 2005. Available: http: //www.whitehouse.gov/news/releases/2005/03/print/20050308–3.html
39. Franklin Delano Roosevelt, *First Inaugural Address*, March 4, 1933.
40. Michel de Montaigne, 1580, *Essays, Book I*.
41. Francis Bacon, *De Augmentis Scientiarum, Book II, Fortitudo*, 1623.
42. Arthur Wellesley, Duke of Wellington, Notes from conversation with Philip Henry, Earl of Stanhope, November 3, 1831.
43. Henry David Thoreau, *Journal*, September 7, 1851.
44. Courage has been defined as *the ability to do something that frightens one*. Courage is synonymous with *bravery* and *fearlessness* and is the opposite of *cowardice*.
45. C. S. Lewis (1944/1997), *The Unquiet Grave* in Thomas C. Peters, *Simply C.S. Lewis*. Wheaton, IL: Crossway Books
46. Thucydides (455–400 BC), was speaking of the greatness of Athens and how this greatness "was won by men with courage, with knowledge of their duty, and with a sense of honor in actions"—not unlike the greatness of all true democracies, including the United States of America. (*The History of the Peloponnesian War*, 431–413 BC, book II, section 43).

7

The Neoconservative Challenge to the Undergraduate Curriculum

The Case of the Intercollegiate Studies Institute and the American Council for Trustees and Alumni

STEVEN SELDEN

[T]here is growing evidence that many American universities are reneging on their duty to educate. The widespread abandonment of academic standards and moral discipline, the politicization of all aspects of campus life, and the deconstruction of academic disciplines have devastated the traditional mission of the liberal arts curriculum. In too many classrooms, professors teach their students that Western thought is suspect, that Enlightenment ideas are inherently oppressive....
>   WILLIAM J. BENNETT

Choosing the Right College: The Whole Truth About America's 100 Top Schools, Intercollegiate Studies Institute (1998).

Behind the conservative critique of U.S. higher education is a fervent commitment to ideals, to be sure—but there's also a sizable amount of conservative cash. The Bradley, Earhart, Castle Rock, and John M. Olin foundations have contributed lavishly to guidebooks aimed at steering young Americans away from certain colleges and universities and to shaping a public's conception of university life and its curriculum. In addition to presenting their ideas in these publications, conservative critiques of the university can also be found on the pages of the nation's leading newspapers. In reporting on David Horowitz' charge that U.S. universities had been "colonized by 'tenured leftists,'" and sorely in need of an "Academic Bill of Rights," the *New York Times* concluded that the campus culture wars of the 1980s had been resurrected (Zhao, 2004, p. A15). Nevertheless, as with the reports cited above, Horowitz' current work is sponsored. It is underwritten by conservative funding sources including the Bradley, Scaife, Carthage, and Olin foundations. A review of public tax records indicates that between 1986 and 1990, Horowitz has received $950,000 in assistance, with his Center for the Study of Popular Culture receiving over $12 million in support between 1989 and 2002. As this chapter will argue, much of the conservative challenge to the undergraduate curriculum over the past half century has been similarly sponsored.

Readers of the summer 2002 issue of *Daedalus*, for example, would find themselves witness to a colloquy between another sponsored conservative academic, Brookings Institution's Diane Ravitch, and a score of colleagues from across the academic landscape. Ravitch's piece "Education and the Culture Wars" argues that the United States suffers from a crisis of "cultural amnesia." As a noted participant in ongoing curriculum debates, Ravitch queries whether civilized life itself will not be at risk if "we allow our culture to be highjacked by a handful of self-righteous pedagogical censors?" (2002, p. 23). While the piece chastises critics of both the Left and the Right, the author's censure is most strongly directed toward progressive educators. It is that faculty, concerned as they are for epistemological and racial multiplicity, which most threaten the traditional canon.

Professor Ravitch's critique of the undergraduate curriculum is consistent with positions taken for more than half a century by neoconservative activists. It is a position that offers strong support for programs based in texts drawn from the Western literary and historical cannon, while rejecting of what Purdue's Calvin Schrag (1988) has identified as the "postmodern" turn of mind. But these jeremiads are something more. They are part of a discourse sponsored by a network of conservative foundations and their funded activist centers and intellectuals. The following chapter will analyze these interconnections. In tracing the links between conservative funders, sponsored centers, and products created for public consumption, this chapter does not presume a conspiracy, vast or right-wing. Conspirators, should there be any, and there are not, would have hidden their activities far more carefully.

The changes in public policy regarding markets, values, and pedagogy that have taken place over the past three decades rest on common ground shared by four interest groups: neoliberals who reckon that an unregulated market is the most efficient way to achieve just economic development; neoconservatives who like Professor Ravitch argue for a curriculum of high cultural standards and traditional knowledge; authoritarian populists who strive to bring religion into all aspects of public and private life; and the new middle class, a group whose technical skills allow for the management of any social construction (Apple, 2001). While these groups have been fixed into a reasonably unified and powerful political movement, many of their respective beliefs are contradictory. For example, neoliberal free markets can be destructive to the traditional values so highly prized by neoconservatives and authoritarian populists. Nevertheless, with conservative foundation support, they have joined in common cause to reject affirmative action, to transform the content of the undergraduate curriculum, and to define marriage in terms of the sexual orientation of the betrothed.

One might argue, as has Covington (1997), that foundations have undertaken a three-step production model for instituting social change grant making. As analyses of their IRS 990PF reports reveal a first step focusing on the *development of raw materials* through the funding and creation of activist centers, a second in which the *conversion of these intellectual raw materials is turned into products*, and a third in which these products are *marketed* and *distributed* for public consumption (Covington, 1997, p. 5). The chapter turns now to analyses of the products developed by two conservative activist centers in their attempts to influence the undergraduate curriculum.

The Intercollegiate Society for Individualists/Intercollegiate Studies Institute

Attempts to influence the undergraduate curriculum by sponsored conservatives can be traced to 1953, to J. Howard Pew's $1,000 gift to Frank Chodorov for the creation of the libertarian-oriented Intercollegiate Society of Individualists (ISI), and to the person of William F. Buckley (figure 7.1, p. 95). It was Buckley, who would serve as the organization's first president, who had warned of secular humanism's influence on his alma mater in *God and Man at Yale* (1951). While secular humanism has been eclipsed by anxieties regarding multiculturalism and postmodernism, ISI, renamed the Intercollegiate Studies Institute in 1963, remains committed to "limited government, individual liberty, personal responsibility, free enterprise, and Judeo-Christian moral standards" (ISI website). However, it is important to recognize that terms such as Judeo-Christian moral standards are open to various interpretations; they are what some contemporary scholars would refer to as sliding signifiers. For example, ISI's list of the 50 Worst Books of the Twentieth Century (ISI website) includes John Rawls's classic in moral philosophy *A Theory of Justice* (1971). In it Rawls argues that citizens should make social policy as if viewing the future through a "veil of ignorance." Denied access to one's destiny, and wishing to guarantee a secure future, moral actors would likely choose policies that would protect society's least advantaged. Since Rawls's "do unto others" policy seems an expression of Judeo-Christian values, what is the reader to make of the presence of his work on ISI's 50 Worst Books list? One answer is that ISI's definition of morality may focus on individuals not communities, on limited government regardless of the demands of the common good (Altbach, 2002). Having supported those antagonistic to university affirmative action programs, the Bradley, Olin, Earhart, and Scaife foundations go on to support ISI's rejection of a Rawlsian approach to social policy. Between 1985 and 2003, ISI received more than $17.4 million from those foundations and others to influence America's best and brightest (Stefanic and Delgado, 1996; Covington, 1997; Media Transparency).

ISI also focuses its energies on the undergraduate curriculum. In the mid-1990s, after a hurried visit from ISI President T. Kenneth Cribb Texas oil billionaire Lee Bass withdrew a promised $20 million grant from Yale for a program in Western civilization. Bass had been moved to make the gift after hearing Yale's Donald Kagen lament liberalism's destructive impact on New Haven's academic standards. The withdrawal of the grant became a cause celebre for the American Right. Newt Gingrich explained that the funding had been withdrawn because no one at Yale was willing to teach Western civilization (Gingrich, 1995), and *US News & World Report* outlined "How the West Was Lost at Yale" (Leo, 1995, p. 19).

But the questions remain: Had multiculturalists denied Western civilization a place at Yale's high table? Had tenured radicals really limited intellectual discourse topics judged politically correct? The evidence suggests that the answer is no. As is often the case in universities, the delay in assigning faculty to the Western civilization offerings had more to do with budget than with ideology. "[Professor] Kagen urged a small, highly coherent program in which all of the students would take the same classes" (Wilson, 1999, p. 433). But administrators, concerned for the costs of a small cohort-program, balked. It was a time of fiscal retrenchment, and while Dr. Kagen requested new hires, university administrators wanted to reassign faculty from other campus programs. In this context, President Cribb flew to Texas. Although Yale quickly agreed to implement the program as originally conceived, Cribb persuaded Bass to demand the right of veto power over any faculty hires. Faced with this threat to institutional independence, Yale chose to return the money. One should not miss the irony here. Tenured radicals did *not* deny Yale students a program focusing on Western civilization. On the contrary, it was disallowed due to the actions of a well-funded conservative activist organization.

In 1998 ISI continued to focus on the undergraduate curriculum with the publication of its college guide *Choosing the Right College: The Whole Truth About America's Top 100 Schools*. Among those penning dust cover accolades, one finds William Kristol, editor of the conservative *Weekly Standard;* Roger Kimball, author of *Tenured Radicals: How Politics Corrupted Our Higher Education* (1990); Martin Anderson of the Hoover Institution; and conservative activist and author and ex-secretary of Education William J. Bennett. In understanding the intersection between conservative foundations and sponsored scholarship, one should note that Kimball, Anderson, and Bennett had all received Olin Foundation largesse. While these are all principled conservatives, their activism is nonetheless sponsored. Between 1990 and 2000, for example, Bennett received over $900,000 in Olin support through his associations with the Heritage Foundation, the Hudson Institute, and Empower America (Media Transparency). In introducing *Choosing* to its readers, Bennett warns of the dire state of U.S. higher education, typified in his view by "widespread abandonment of academic standards and moral discipline, the politicization of all aspects of campus life, and the deconstruction of academic disciplines." While these forces have "devastated the traditional mission of the liberal arts curriculum" (Wolfe, 1998, p. x), there are still colleges and universities that stand against the tide. The *Choosing*'s reviewers hold St. John's College and its rejection of "politically correct" policies as such an institution. Additionally, the reader learns that St. John's "doesn't have to deal with speech codes, hiring or student body quotas, and the desire of a misguided administration to teach the latest ideological trends in order to rank high on someone else's ill conceived list" (Wolfe, 1998, p. 501). Surely there are reasoned positions that can be taken on either side of these difficult issues, but this seems a rather brittle rendering of race. After all, the U.S. Supreme Court in its *Bakke* decision found quotas in hiring and college admissions illegal. And the *Choosing*'s hostility to them seems somehow misplaced; no university may legally institute a policy of quotas. Perhaps ISI's hostility reflects a warranted belief that affirmative action policies, unlike quotas, are constitutionally offensive. While this position may best describe the guide's orientation, the reader should recognize that this taking of offense is well sponsored. And further, the empirical evidence that would lead to such an affront seems lacking. In any case, the very same foundations whose proxies have challenged affirmative action in the nation's highest court also support its rejection on the pages of *Choosing the Right College*.

National Alumni Forum/American Council of Trustees and Alumni

We turn now to a second activist center, the National Alumni Forum (NAF), to its transformation into the American Council of Trustees and Alumni (ACTA), and to its director, Lynne V. Cheney. While in government service during the Reagan administration, Dr. Cheney used the bully pulpit of the Secretariat of the National Endowment for the Humanities (NEH) to present a caustic critique the undergraduate curriculum. In *Telling the Truth* (1992), Cheney charged that the humanities had been taken over by radical feminist Marxists who found the traditional literary and historical canon hateful, rejected objectivity and the notion of truth, and used the university as a platform for their political beliefs. Propaganda was their pedagogy, and they threatened higher education from within. The only hope was being to bring *external* pressure on the university, and an organization was needed to undertake that task. As is often the case when administrations change, appointees move from the government to the policy community. Thus, in 1994 with assistance from ISI, the National Alumni Forum (NAF) was created with Dr. Cheney as its head.

Rather than focus on students and their parents, as did ISI, the NAF concentrates on "the mobiliz[ation] of alumni on behalf of academic freedom and excellence on college campuses" (www.goacta.org). In 1998, again with Cheney serving as director, NAF was transformed into the American Council of Trustees and Alumni (ACTA). While the name changed, the focus remained the same; ACTA is committed to defending Western canonical literature and historical knowledge against the perceived threat of liberal higher education pedagogues and policies. Between 1996 and 2001, NAF/ACTA received $3,458,156 from Olin, Bradley, Scaife, Castle Rock, and Earhart, in efforts to reshape the university curriculum (Hohneke, 2003). And ACTA continues to focus on motivating conservative alumni to engage in curricular matters. Describing a highly politicized university, it warns that

> The main threat to academic freedom is from political intolerance on campus.... [And] alumni and trustees must make sure our colleges and universities remain forums for open debate. [Alumni] want to support their colleges, but they are often shut out of the discussion. This organization will serve as a voice for interested and concerned alums.
>
> (www.goacta.org)

A commitment to open debate is central to the academic enterprise, but it is by no means the private property of advocates of any single political hue. Those concerned for civil liberties across the political spectrum from CATO to ACLU demand that the academy remain an open forum. Nevertheless, in promoting the claim that the openness is needed for a healthy academic community is at peril, both ACTA have created, marketed, and distributed a number of funded products including *Defending Civilization: How Our Universities Are Failing America and What Can Be Done About It* (2001).

In 2001, ACTA focused its concerns for the putative crisis besetting the university on particular interpretations of canonical history in the curriculum "to support and defend the study of American history and civics and of Western Civilization" (Martin and Neal, 2001, p. i). With financial support from the Randolph Foundation, the William and Karen Tell Foundation, and Jane H. Fraser of The Stuttering Foundation, its first report was published with the polemical title *Defending Civilization: How Our Universities Are Failing America and What Can Be Done About It* (2001). *Defending Civilization* reports that while 92% of post-9/11 Americans "favor military force even if casualties occur" and rally "behind the

President wholeheartedly," the university was out of step with the majority" (p. 1). Its faculty espoused "moral equivocation . . . [and] explicit condemnations of America" (p. 1), with discussions concerning terrorism, captured by faculty who "BLAME AMERICA FIRST" (p. 3, caps in original). Based on such unsubstantiated rhetorical flourishes, the report goes on to recommend that consensus be created through revision of the curriculum—redirecting the undergraduate course of study for political purposes. Supporting Dr. Cheney's charge that "we need to know, in a war, exactly what is at stake," the report demands that "all colleges and universities . . . adopt strong core curricula that include rigorous, broad-based courses on the great works of Western Civilization" (p. 7). The report continues that while the nation had come together in patriotic reaction against the horrors of 9/11, "the fact remains, that academe is the only sector of American society that is distinctly divided in response." Again, absent supporting evidence, the report charges that "expressions of moral relativism are a staple of academic life in this country and an apparent symptom of an educational system that has increasingly suggested that Western Civilization is the primary source of the world's ills . . ." (pp. 4–5).

Upon reflection, there is something deeply troubling about this form of argument as the events of September 11, 2001, metastasize from the United States to Southeast Asia (Van Natta, 2004). It is not simply that ACTA makes these charges without evidence. Rather, it contrasts its presumed *academic* position with a supposedly *political* position held by university faculty. It is a kind of apples and oranges argument ("our positions are academic, theirs are political") in which the putative faculty position is framed as being unpatriotic. While there are principled reasons for making the Western canon central to the curriculum, basing the argument on anecdotes and the claim that one's opponents are treasonous, seems both illogical and untoward.

In the spring of 2001 ACTA was selected by Governor Jeb Bush to instruct 145 of Florida's newly appointed university and college trustees (American Council of Trustees and Alumni, 2001, p. 1). Absent a copy of their trustee-training manual, one cannot describe the content of these instructional programs. However, having reviewed ACTA's depiction of campus dissent in *Defending Civilization*, we may anticipate that their recommendations will include strong support for the Western canon and strong antagonism toward critical pedagogy.

Conclusion

Over the past half century, ISI and ACTA have received more than $19.9 million for the production and distribution of neoconservative campus guides and curriculum evaluations (figure 7.2, p. 95). With support from the Olin, Bradley, Earhart, and Castle Rock Foundations, these centers have developed projects designed to influence public perception of the university faculty and the undergraduate curriculum. *Choosing the Right College* (ISI), *The Shakespeare File* (ACTA), and *Defending Civilization* (ACTA) are all part of an attempt at a broader conservative restoration.

The college guide and curriculum analysis reviewed above share common themes. They define the liberal arts as content rather than process. They follow Matthew Arnold's dictum that undergraduates should have contact with "the best that has been thought and said," and they offer strong support for prescribed curricula such as those offered by St. Johns College and the University of Chicago. But they do not present deeply reasoned arguments for any of these positions or recommendations. In the place of such coherent discussions one often finds critiques that are both strident and anecdotal. Generally absent substantiation, they present unsettling views of faculty loyalty to the university and the state. The university faculty, depicted as a kind of "fifth column," is often portrayed as determined to destroy the academy from within. At the pedagogical level, faculty are said to disregard and deconstruct the Western canon; in the face of national threat and war, they are charged with disloyalty. The reports' views on race are equally disturbing. The academy, if one is to believe the materials reviewed above, disregards merit in admissions and hiring and is typified by racial set asides and quotas. And authors such as Shakespeare are disrespected for reasons unspecified. These views, as with those on faculty loyalty, are presented without empirical evidence. They give a picture of a university that very few of today's faculty and students would recognize. But depict it they do. Given the above analysis, one might wonder if these sponsored products were ever designed to engage faculty and the public in a reasoned debate regarding the meaning of knowledge, the state, or morality. Under careful review it seems more likely that these publications were to serve as what philosophers would call ceremonial slogans. That is, the guides and evaluations were designed to elicit an emotional rather than an intellectual response. And as we know, such slogans are designed for affiliation, not clarification. In these times of a deeply fractured polity, providing the public with reasoned discussion rather than slogans would have seemed a more helpful tool for resolving policy debates regarding the undergraduate curriculum. They did not provide such reasoned analysis.

While this chapter does not support the general thrust of the conservative project, it nevertheless recognizes considerable merit in the neoconservative position. As Catherine Stimpson, dean of NYU's Graduate School of Arts and Sciences, notes, the neoconservative plea is for a university curriculum centered on great works of literature and history strives for commendable goals (Stimpson, 2002, p. 37). Whether William Buckley, William Bennett, Lynne Cheney, or Diane Ravitch make that plea, that hoped-for curriculum does focus on worthy outcomes. That is, their plea is much like Stimpson's. It is for curricula that will "create national cohesion, democratic order, and some ability to understand The Other" (Stimpson, 2002, p. 37).

Alas, and this may not be encouraging news for neoconservative academics, while they were undertaking their assault on the undergraduate curriculum, the intellectual terrain shifted beneath their feet. As Purdue University's Calvin Schrag notes, liberal learning found itself in a "postmodern world" (Schrag, 1988, p. 1). In art, postmodernism is antirealist; in literature it is suspicious of the rules of literary language; in science it is concerned for "instabilities," for shifting paradigms; in philosophy, postmodernism is antifoundationalist and suspicious of theory (Schrag, 1988, p. 4). As Schrag puts it, postmodernism is "more like an attitude . . . a way of seeing the world and acting within it [than an easily defined area of study such as physics]" (Schrag, 1988, p. 4). This has to be profoundly unsettling to neoconservative sensibilities. Indeed, one might conclude that it was against just this attitude that the sponsored neoconservative challenge was launched a half century ago.

The view described by Schrag, while unsettling to many conservatives, can be remarkably useful to members of the twenty-first-century academy. As Stimpson points out, it can assist in the creation of "a curriculum for students whose complex sense of citizenship may simultaneously include loyalty to a place of origin, the American nation-state, a faith, and a global society that connects its citizens economically and electronically" (Stimpson, 2002, p. 37). These are splendid goals for the undergraduate course of study, worthy of support from conservatives and progressives alike. They are goals capable of successfully responding to the changed intellectual landscape on which we find ourselves, of developing the deep humanity of our students, and of responding creatively to reasoned conservative assaults on the undergraduate curriculum.

Note

A more extensive version of this paper can be found in Selden, S., "Who's Paying for the Culture Wars?" *Academe* (www.aaup.org/publications/Academe/2005/05so/05soseld.htm), accessed on September 9, 2006.

References

Altbach, P. G. (Fall 2002). Farewell to the Common Good. *International Educator,* 13–17.
American Council of Trustees and Alumni (2001). Florida Joins Accountability Movement, *Inside Academe* 6(3) (Spring/Summer), 1.
Apple, M. W. (2001). *Educating the "Right" Way.* New York and London: Routledge.
Buckley, W. F. (1951). *God and Man at Yale: The Superstitions of Academic Freedom.* Chicago: Regnery.

Cheney, L. V. (1992). *Telling the Truth: A Report on the State of the Humanities in Higher Education.* Washington, DC: National Endowment for the Humanities.

Covington, S. (1997). *Moving a Public Policy Agenda: The Strategic Philanthropy of Conservative Foundations, A Report From the National Committee for Responsive Philanthropy.* Washington, DC: National Committee for Responsive Philanthropy.

Gingrich, N. (1995). *To Renew America.* New York: HarperCollins.

Hohneke, T. (2003). The Conservative Restoration and the Undergraduate Curriculum: Tracing the Financial Roots and Policy Initiatives of the American Council of Trustees and Alumni. Unpublished paper, University of Maryland College Park.

Intercollegiate Studies Institute (2003). http://www.isi.org/about_isi.html. Retrieved on October 1, 2006.

Kimball, R. (1998). *Tenured Radicals: How Politics Has Corrupted Our Higher Education.* Chicago: Ivan R. Dee Publishers.

Leo, J. (1995, April 3). How the West Was Lost at Yale. *US News & World Report,* 7.

Martin, J. L., and Neal, A. D. (2001). *Defending Civilization: How Our Universities Are Failing America and What Can Be Done about It.* Washington, DC: American Council of Trustees and Alumni.

Media Transparency. Retrieved from http://www.mediatransparency.org. Retrieved on October 1, 2006. [S1]

Ravitch, D. (Summer 2002). Education and the Culture Wars. *Daedalus: Journal of the American Academy of Arts and Sciences,* 131(3), 5–21.

Rawls, J. (1971). *A Theory of Justice.* Cambridge: Harvard University Press.

Schrag, C. O. (1988). Liberal Learning in the Postmodern World. Paper presented to the Purdue University Phi Beta Kappa graduation (mimeo copy).

Stefanic, J., and Delgado, R. (1996). *No Mercy: How Conservative Think Tanks and Foundations Changed America's Social Agenda.* Philadelphia: Temple University Press.

Stimpson, C. R. (Summer 2002). The Culture Wars Continue. *Daedalus: Journal of the American Academy of Arts and Sciences,* 131, 36–40.

Van Natta, D. (2004, April 18). A World Made More Dangerous as Terrorism Spreads. *New York Times,* section 4, p. 1.

Wilson, J. K. (1999). The Canon and the Curriculum. In P. Altbach, R. Berdahl, and J. Gumport (Eds.), *American Higher Education in the Twenty-First Century: Social, Political, and Economic Changes.* Baltimore: The John Hopkins University Press.

Wolfe, G. (Ed.). (1998). *Choosing the Right College: The Whole Truth about America's 100 Top Schools.* Grand Rapids: William B. Eerdmans Publishing Company.

Zhao, Y. (2004, April 3). Taking the Liberalism out of Liberal Arts. *New York Times,* p. A1.

Organization (Year Created)	Intercollegiate Soc. of Individualists (1953) Intercollegiate Studies Institute (1963)	National Alumni Forum (1994) American Council for Trustees and Alumni (1997)
Leadership	Frank Chodorov William F. Buckley	Lynne V. Cheney Jerry L. Martin Anne D. Neal
Foundation Funding Sources	Bradley Castle Rock Earhart McKenna Olin Scaife	Bradley Castle Rock Malcolm Frazer Earhart Olin Sarah Scaife Wm. And Karen Tell
Selected Products	*Choosing the Right College: The Whole Truth About America's Top Schools (1998-2005)*	*Defending Civilizations: How Our Universities Are Failing America And What Can Be Done About It* (2001)
Financial Support Year(s)	$17,489,600 (1985-2003)	$2,502,300 (1994-2003)

FIGURE 7.1. Conservative Foundations, Funded Activist Centers, Their Products, and the Undergraduate Curriculum.

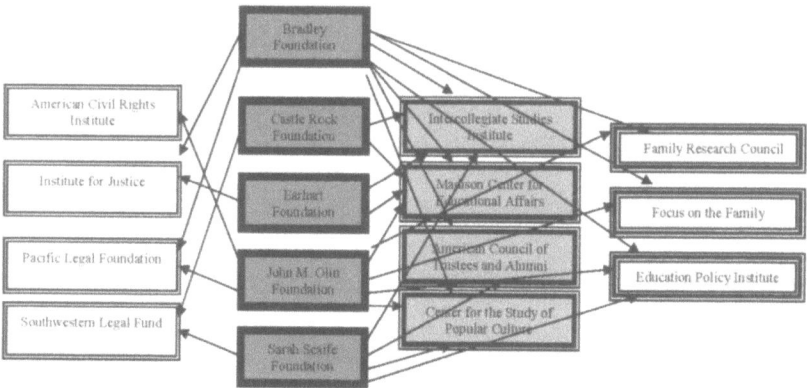

FIGURE 7.2. Linking Conservative Foundation Funding with Activist Social Neoconservative, Academic Neoconservative, and Authoritarian Populist Centers.

Part III

Finding Meaning in the Four Freedoms

In 1984, Robert Bellah revisited Alexis de Tocqueville's ideas on the individual actions that lead Americans on their unique nation-building journey. *Habits of the Heart* became the words that represented the unique aspect of American individualism. As a people, we interpret national and international problems through our own eyes and experiences. Although, FDR's Four Freedoms were meant as a foundational declaration of democratic and human rights for all, the final four chapters examine them from individual perspectives. This is appropriate as ultimately democratic societies provide opportunities for individual growth through internalization of the values espoused by the Four Freedoms.

David M. Callejo Pérez offers an autobiographical journey as a teacher in an inner city school where Social Studies becomes a space to visit the Four Freedoms, specifically the freedom from fear as students and teacher candidly discuss race and its implications on the minds of Americans. The chapter offers insights on how revisiting the past offers criticism and choices for the future.

Jennifer Deets' chapter is an account of her dilemma between support of democratic public schools and its opportunities; and a curriculum which no longer is responsive to her values of family. Deets treasures the home as an integral part of a child's life. She understood that schools were a continuation of home values and in turn it helped shape the values learned within the home. However, changes in the relationship between school and community have forced parents to elect home schooling as the most appropriate option to teach values of democracy, freedom, and ethics as understood in her home. The chapter reflects the agony of a professional educator faced with this difficult choice.

Donn C. Worgs and Leon D. Caldwell write a historical/philosophical piece that ties together freedom/liberation and education from an African-American viewpoint. Beginning with the post Civil War period and ending with the post-Civil Rights era they question the notion of self-governance taken for granted by most Americans as missing within African-American society. They see the problem as twofold, one the reliance on education that hinders access for Blacks and second, and more vicious how politics have undermined the opportunities for participation of Blacks in the democratic process.

Judith J. Slater takes us on a personal journey that examines how language shapes individual perception. Slater writes that understanding the relationship between language and the internalization of ideas provides an opportunity for the manipulation of the individual. Citing the examples from the social-political landscape, she demonstrates why the individual must assert personal judgment or succumb to those who would mislead citizens through language manipulation.

References

Bellah, R., Et. Al (1984). *Habits of the heart*. Berkeley, CA: University of California Press.

8
Social Studies

High School History as Racial Text

DAVID M. CALLEJO PÉREZ

In 1995, I decided to work in the north side of Miami, Florida. I grew up in the affluent Coral Gables in southern Miami. When I began teaching, my mind was littered with thoughts of violence, riots, and failing schools. I began in October where on my first day I was assigned surplus students that other social studies teachers did not want in their classes. Two periods of world history and three of U.S. history were given to me; ninth graders in world history were taught in the back of an auditorium that seated 150 students. The two sections contained forty-five students each, not uncommon for an inner city school. The U.S. history eleventh graders were a much different story. Each class had twenty students, aided by what one administrator told me was the high dropout rate for freshmen, which for him was a positive sign—"less problems, you know," as he used to always tell me. I quickly figured why we never gave kids textbooks or school supplies. The dropout rate was so high that when students left with books, it cost the school a fortune. Barely unpacked on the first day, I was asked by a Haitian eleventh grader, JaSheena, if we are the land of liberty and democracy, why is our world full of hate, racism, and injustice?" I remember saying to myself, "holy shit what did I get into!" I said, "Why do you ask?" "Because you are white and from Mississippi so you must know about racism," quickly followed. I interrupted, "I'm actually from here, just went to school at the University of Mississippi." "But if you're White . . . ," she continued. "Well, I'm actually Cuban, and . . ." Interrupting, she scanned me and said, "well you're not Black like Mr. Ortiz!" I told her Cubans were very diverse, and in fact most Cubans I knew were white. I immediately realized that she had rarely left her neighborhood. She in fact had only gone downtown once on the Metro Rail, "to go to court" cause my uncle...."

What did I step into? I remembered social studies as the subject where we learned dates and names of famous Americans. I believed that this debate was not to have occurred until graduate school, but I was faced with the question and addressed the only way I knew how. The social studies classroom is the place where we have to critically examine our history in order to make sense of our present. American history is dotted with many interesting debates. However, none is more powerful than race and/or slavery. Its impact is seen in every aspect of our lives, from the U.S. Constitution; the Amendments (13, 14, and 15 specifically deal with slavery and human rights); to three cases every eleventh grader can recite: Dred Scott, *Plessy v. Ferguson*, and *Brown v. Board of Education, Topeka, Kansas*. In the 1940s and 1950s, as the nation was gripped in the debate of what to do about World War II, the Holocaust, the Nuclear Age, and Human Rights, Franklin Delano Roosevelt fostered hope in an inconsequential speech that addressed four basic freedoms: (1) speech and expression; (2) of worship of God in his own way; (3) freedom from want; and (4) freedom from fear. I believe that the most important question rests in the fourth freedom, fear. I believe that this is where social studies belongs in terms of what its purpose is within the school curriculum. Fear resulted from not knowing, seeing, or embracing our past. In other words, the experience that is most crucial to a democracy is birthing of difficult conversations nurtured within freedom of speech. What follows below is my personal account of such an experience, explained through a simple lesson couched in that history which we have fully addressed in our public schools: Race and the Identity of America.

Committing to Community

I was interested in relating the question of race and the conflict it held within to U.S. history. It was already October, and we were beginning to study the antebellum (1820–1860) period. I had a Master's in history and began classes in curriculum studies in Miami. I proposed a curriculum that would drive the school year by examining our racial past and approach the conflict between the races through curriculum change in the public schools. I began with Benedict Anderson's (1991) concept of imagined communities to explore the concept of cultural identity. He described imagined community as *imagined* because, although the members of the community might not know each other, "in the minds of each lives the image of their communion" (Anderson, 1991, p. 6). It is a *community*, because, "regardless of the actual inequality and exploitation that may prevail in each, the nation is always conceived as a deep, horizontal comradeship" (Anderson, 1991, p. 7). Addressing our race requires individualizing it within the larger study of U.S. history. First, we had to admit that we live with the duality of espoused equality and freedom while practicing racial stratification (racism). George Fredrickson (1982), Edmund Morgan (1975), and T. H. Breen (1980) agreed that racism is separated into two categories: (1) outward action of a person and (2) personal ideology. Ideological racism came from our European background, Western superiority, and "White Man's Burden." Racism's outward action comes from our history of slavery.

Society, especially in the United States is concerned with place and past, especially regional and racial identities as witnessed by the rise of genealogy searches and the attempt at recreating our immigrant pasts. Schools, busy with acculturation and assimilation, do not honestly deal with those problems in their curricula. As the onus of civil rights, individual racial identity was methodically placed at the forefront of U.S. culture before community equity, creating spaces for the women's, Chicano, and other similar movements. As a nation we have always faced problems of race and had to invent new forms of expression from which to define the new meanings created as a result. Louis Castenell and William Pinar state that it is an "understatement to observe that issues of race are paramount in contemporary curriculum debates in the public sphere" (Castenell and Pinar, 1993, p. 2). They suggest that curriculum is "racial text" because debates about what we teach youngsters are "debates over who we perceive ourselves to be, and how we will represent that identity, including what remains as 'left over,' as 'difference'" (p. 2). Curriculum as race, text, and identity implies understanding the "American national identity, and vice versa" as racial text (p. 2). Race and identity are terms constantly changing; one grows out of the individual's past, as say, for example, "Black" from slavery, whereas identity comes from how the individual deals with her past, and what role society assigns that past.

As the repression of individual identity was lifted by social changes, so too did schools respond, allowing marginalized groups to identify with symbols separate from the dominant social culture. Thus, African Americans in a quest for their African identity no longer saw themselves as extremities of Europeans, ultimately leading to a new definition of self as African. In our nation, the African American individual was always subject to an autobiographical experience that would attempt at separation from a dominant political and social structure that oppressed individual freedom and identity. Therein lays the appeal of the character's struggle for independence in current society. Second, the individual search for her identity in terms of the larger base of knowledge and tradition comes to fruition in attempts to discover themselves as black or feminine or worthy in the face of the closed society of the United States. The release finds a receptacle in marginalized groups, particularly women and persons of color. Third, schooling has traditionally marginalized the importance of these groups as well as providing a place for these groups to exist. In the literature, they find there is no place for them that others too have tried and become ostracized for their attempts to become free by the social order.

Schooling is an institutional representation of the society that encompasses it. The nature of the change in schools as a response to its social milieu is the repression of African Americans in our society has not been properly addressed. As curriculum is nationalized and standardized, it has excluded aspects of individual identity, forcing marginalization through the public policy of integration. Although the media tells us that we have similar needs and wants, Castenell and Pinar believe that "all Americans are racialized beings; knowledge of who we have been, who we are, and who we will become is a story or text we will construct" (Castenell and Pinar, 1993, p. 8). There is hope that within the schooling and its curriculum there are still gray spaces where individuals can address the concepts of social justice and equality. We can educate learners through the use of critical questioning. Taking this into consideration, I decided to construct a curriculum of self-discovery and identity. I began with a framework and hoped students would fill in the blanks. Slavery and the study of its role in the United States would lead to discovery on different levels for us as a group. The first level would be to construct a thematic curriculum around one theme leading to discovery of specific factual knowledge in history. The second level would hopefully provide connections between the past and the present and lead to analysis of individual students and their experiences. Last, a level based on the creation of a language to cut across boundaries of self-discovery to live out the ideas of diversity within society, and ultimately affect change if that cliché could be used. In a sense it was a search for hope in education.

The path through curriculum must take a real and personal analysis of slavery, creating a conversation between history and the students' experiences. Using the historiography of slavery, I decided to deconstruct the history of the United States through the use of three dominant slavery historiography paradigms: (1) passive resistance; (2) economic; and (3) autobiographical. Nicholas Onuf (1989) offers one example in creating a public knowledge basis for criticism. In his attempt to rescue the field of international relations, he wished to break from the boundaries of existing disciplines (Onuf, 1989, pp. 11–12). In Onuf's view, fundamental argument is conducted in the social sciences by reinterpreting classical works. This undertaking cannot be judged in absolute terms. As one wades through what seems to be a random selection of texts, Onuf points to the primary characteristic of modernity, a pluralistic complexity in which competing skills and organization produce specialism and differentiation, of which the state is one such organization.

In a similar manner, our zest to form counternarratives and discredit structural models of schools and curriculum, specifically Ralph Tyler, have awakened a dangerous neoconservative response to the attack of a perceived viable model of schools accepted as legitimate (because of its accountability factor) without offering a real alternative (Apple 1996; Giroux, 1988). If as a field, curriculum makers, including teachers, do not heed to Onuf's warning, we leave ourselves without an entree to the institutions we are supposed to change.

In this schism of disciplines, where theoretical approaches of curriculum and not aligned with models of accountability, I attempted to bring together the theory of equality, with an equal praxis, through language by building a curriculum approach that teaches learners about slavery, and hopefully, helps them to critically approach the issue of racism, free of constraints placed on them by standardized curriculum. The curricular example is an effort to link traditional Tylerian approaches, used by schools today, to postmodern paradigms, fleshing out a spirituality of faith in connection to history and our ability to change its interpretation. For example, David Giddens (1976, 1991) sees the individual as an active participant in social life and not a mere bystander in search for identity. He is also critical of the poststructuralists' neglect of the structural aspects of society and their binding effects on action and attributes self-efficacy to the individual in dealing with the search for identity. The broad-brush stroke I have used above to label the poststructuralists is not fair; I mean to attack a specific notion of identity that is placed upon the learner, specifically without their consent. For example, I could construct a curricular plan to be followed, already creating what I believe the identity of African American students should be like based on my experiences, but that would defeat the purpose of having students create individual and different identities based on a common history. However, notions of deconstructionist theory do shed light on a grassroots approach to curriculum design that to subvert top-down approaches to curriculum. Expectations for change exist in the process of living the curriculum, but they are underlined with the hope that students' faith in the relationship among them, the curriculum, and me will result in the creation of common experiences.

Deconstructing History

The first step of creating this curriculum is to build from a deconstructionist point of view. As Derrida (1978) intended, deconstruction is the rigorous critique of the fundamental axioms of Western thought, with the purpose of exposing its biases via an analysis of the contradictions of major Western philosophical texts. This process is not only negative (destruction of the axioms) but also positive (reconstruction of the axioms in a novel manner). The idea is to take the individual out of her societal reality, explore her I (self), then examine society without the individual. Once the two have been examined, they will then be reconstructed to form a new reality.

The curriculum links our past and future through our present. The past existed, and the future will exist but their reality relies on their relation to the present. Culler (1976/1979) states that "the future is an anticipated presence and the past a former presence" (p. 162). Derrida's view allows for a reexamination of the entire project of modern epistemology. It is possible to deconstruct the truth claims of writers by analyzing how they employ rhetorical and self-privileging strategies in the construction of their truth claims (Derrida, 1981). The implication of this quest for certainty is the search for foundations, that is, the establishment of secure principles from which we can build a conceptual edifice that can capture the chaotic world of facts and contingencies. Derrida contends that the history of Western metaphysics (metaphysics of presence) is a constant search for foundations. The question follows then is how to allow for each individual, given her past, to retain her individual experience and thus change her future?

Schools have been places where society is perpetuated, where conformity is taught, and where deviance is discouraged. They inculcate children into learning the norms and values of the dominant culture—first, through emulation (most powerful, where the child believes what she is learning is good); second, through diplomacy (where the school tries to prove to the child that school is good); third, through manipulation (by bribing the child with a diploma); fourth, by threatening force (making the child learn what is taught, ill-equipping the child for thinking); and lastly, by force (where the child is miseducated, through a deficit model of education) (Brantlinger, 2004). This cultural hegemony can be overcome by exposing the history of the past and reality of one's present, not one the school has prechosen.

Since postmodernism has revealed "the truth" to be an outcome of power configurations (Foucault, 1977, 1980), linguistically biased and arbitrary philosophical hierarchies (Derrida, 1981, 1982; Rorty, 1979), or self-referential language games (Lyotard, 1984), there is a tendency for them to conclude that modern conceptualizations of truth and reality are outmoded concepts, since both truth and reality appear to be the products of discourse, there is little need to write as if discourse must originate in them. Thus, one viable option for theory is to recognize itself as a form of literature and practice poetics or polemics, because in the literary model, theory no longer needs to defend its claim of representing the real—for the real is always brought into being by language (Rorty, 1982). It is an attempt to end the hegemonic control on truth by science in schooling.

Actor accounts are considered as legitimate as contrived and secondhand conceptual schemes of traditional philosophers. Reality that is constructed, interpreted, and acted by human beings is a legitimate source for curriculum. It is the role of the phenomenological/hermeneutic approach to explain how everyday knowledge is created and maintained, not to assess its validity or truthfulness (Berger and Luchmann, 1967, p. 3).

If we trust that "analytic thinking of modernity must be replaced by critical historicity," and the "linear model divides time into the past, present and future, and as a result removes any autobiographical connection to the historical events" (Slattery, 1995, p. 41), then what are we searching for? In my context, empowerment was the ability to recognize my awareness and harness it into participation within the larger society (Freire, 1970). We are a product of past, and once we realize that, then we can examine our present, make corrections, and change our future. Karl Popper (1984/1992) offers an alternative position that I considered, especially when balancing the delicate scales between transmission of culture and standardized curriculum in U.S. history and the social reconstructionist view of the subject expounded by Harold Rugg and George Counts. Popper believed that knowledge was the search for truth, that is, "the search for objective truth" (p. 4). His turn on the power of language is a little different from the postmodernists. Popper is a phenomenologist, in the tradition of Hegel (Pinkard, 1994), who like Hegel believes that human language is descriptive statements (with self-expression and symbolism), and we have added argumentative functions (a way to check our own theories for the objective truth). This leads to criticism, a conscious choice of theories over natural selection. We can find and eradicate our errors consciously. This is the first step in the beginning of human knowledge. "There is no knowledge without rational criticism, criticism is the service of the search for truth" (Popper, 1984/1992, p. 21).

If "we can predict the future, but not well, we cannot see the unforeseeable consequences of our actions" (Popper 1984/1992, p. 28), and then how do we build a curriculum model for studying slavery that satisfies public schools accountability and celebrates individual experiences? Teachers must allow for learners to learn through the questioning of the facts. Knowledge is the search for truth. There is no criterion of truth; "even when we have reached the truth we can never be certain of it. There is a rational criterion for progress in the search for truth. Science is a critical activity" (p. 38). If we are convinced that we are in search for a truth, not a metanarrative truth, but an individual hermeneutical experienced truth that will lead to empowerment, not through sociopolitical means, but empowerment through intellectual liberation, then the proper method to use is to study the system and be critical of it. Studying the system means knowing it, using it, and understanding it. Criticism implies the ability to know that the system exists physically, consciously, and as an idea in an individual's mind. In order to make the leap from the physical to the ideological, individuals must step out of their social system and observe it objectively from an external perspective. This privilege is only accorded to those who are able to critically think and question; this in my mind was connected to social class and education. There are two luxuries that I live with. Questions must extend beyond how others feel. They must deal with how an individual feels as he/she is involved within the educational system. Even though our answers are unique, the questions we ask are similar because they deal with our survival and our ability to be heard. If a group of individuals asks similar questions about a system, even if they come from different backgrounds, they will be able to understand where they fit within the larger narrative.

When an educator is dealing with curriculum today, she must ask how her work will limit or extend freedom. For example, I knew that the study of American slavery has been very difficult for historians. The question has centered on whether slavery begot racism or racism begot slavery. In other words, was racism a defensive mechanism to justify slavery, or because slaves were black, was it easier to enslave them? That debate drives the historical field, but as educators we need to acknowledge that slavery happened, and whether slavery or racism came first is not as important for us as the lingering effect it has left in the form of racial stratification.

Creating the Curriculum

The most difficult step was selecting a path that allowed for individuals to seek change within themselves. First was to use criteria that defined our problem. Second, how would we implement the curriculum? Criteria came from Popper's (1972) ideas about objective knowledge (model for the learner to become critical of his situation). The decision for implementation was extremely difficult, since it required a rejection of the teacher education paradigm, seeing education as a place where a single paradigm of learning was perpetuated (Illich, 1971), and how I would live within the school's bureaucratic hegemony and live out this search for race and identity with my students. Once we could reject these paradigms as absolutes and recognize that there is more, then learners and teachers could move toward examining the conflict American slavery has engendered between the ideology of freedom and equality and the practice of racial stratification.

Slave Historiography Models: Setting the Tone for Creation

The historiography of the study of slavery offers three viable paradigms that when synthesized form one positive critical image that includes a synoptic view of slave society; counternarratives by the slaves; and place of slave society within its context. Herbert Aptheker (1943/1989) and Kenneth Stampp (1956) viewed blacks as active members of their society. Aptheker attacked the idea of the "sambo," a dumb, child-like being that did not know any better about their conditions. He discovered that there were 200 uprisings or talks of uprisings among slaves. Stampp believed that Aptheker was exaggerating, although he found that passive resistance was very common among the slaves. These two historians regarded slaves as active participants within slavery, using the system to their advantage. These two historians also placed slavery within the larger context of America, as a system that was an important aspect of our history.

Second, Robert Fogel and Stanley Engerman's (1974) *Time on the Cross* was an economic take on slavery as profitable and of slaves as good workers. Their model coincided with Marxist historian Eric Williams (1964/1966) who believed slavery was an economic system that naturally died when it ceased to be profitable, not because it was inhumane. Engerman and Fogel saw blacks as motivated workers, who equated work with rewards. They viewed slavery as economic (not social) and slaves as commodities. They also asserted that slaves had as much to lose or gain as their masters because their situation depended on how much money they made for their master. The relationships were reciprocal. There was always the risk that if a kind master went broke, the slaves could be sold to a harsher master, or vice versa, by not working, they could cause a harsh master to lose money and force him to sell them to another master.

The third paradigm is led by critical theorists such as Eugene Genovese (1974), who tried to concentrate on the interpersonal relationships between the masters and the slaves. This group has also been joined by feminists such as Elizabeth Fox-Genovese (1988), who explores the intimate relationships that house slaves formed with mistresses. African American scholars, such as Barbara J. Fields (1982, pp. 283–313), have also explored these relationships. Fields states that to study the black experience of slavery, the historian must be black. This is the only way she can understand the plight of the slave. She argues that race and class come together in the American slave system: black is associated with the lower class. Race is an ideological state, that is, blacks are enslaved because they are black. This third group of historians examines the role of the slave as an active thinking member of a larger society by concentrating on dyadic relationships of slaves and masters and by studying the role of women within the patriarchic society giving both the slaves and women a discourse.

These three paradigms are launching points for our journey. I named the first paradigm passive resistance. This paradigm allows the individual to make a personal connection with slavery as more than a concept. The second paradigm is the economic system. This paradigm allows the individual to view slavery as a dehumanizing institution. This is complicated because the individual is being asked to look at a social institution without seeing the humanity. In this I hope to have the learners make a connection between present-day American institutions and how the past (the institution of slavery) has affected them. The third paradigm is the autobiographical notions of identity. The autobiographical paradigm allows each learner to realize their potential and meet the conflict between their story and that which is told in schools. George Counts believed that at the base of American education "there is a profound faith in the potentialities of the individual man" (Counts, 1971, p. 12). This faith is what I was hoping to recover with a curriculum around the three paradigms examining slavery as a central institution that drove the conflict between our espoused theory of equality and the pervasive racial stratification that dominates our relationships. The unifying force that will carry this massive curriculum effort is democracy.

Designing the Curriculum

Curriculum design in schooling has followed a linear approach. In one way or another, curriculum design has changed very little in the past fifty years. As a young teacher, I decided to create a curriculum for the students addressing their needs and remain below the radar of the school administrator under strict orders to keep everyone on the task of passing the basic skills test. School curriculum seeks to create a context that sets learners in categories through the use of testing and rigid assignments to particular notions of learning. Jurgen Habermas (1992) stated that individuals must be rescued from complete absorption into the particular contexts in which she is always embedded.

In *Dare the Schools Build a New Social Order?* (1932), George Counts required teachers be leaders of social revolutions that would change and improve democratic America. Mao Tse Tung also used teachers in order to permanently change his society (Burns, 1978). I understood the importance of teaching and our influence, but where the line between creating experiences and spaces, and indoctrinating was, replacing one philosophy for another, was still a mystery. This, I thought, was the trap Paolo Freire warned educators against (1970). Yet, I was not aware where my role as guide began and ended or where my students saw themselves as learners. I figured we would discover these things together. The uncertainty I felt was echoed by Robert Donmoyer (1991) in describing "improvisational, informal, or responsive teaching" (p. 101). Improvisational teaching and learning would be our organization, and in these uncertainties we would find our process. I felt no fear, why, "I was the baseball coach!" Kids respected me. It was an interesting notion, an ironic one, that a social studies teacher coached. However, in this case it offered me the freedom to be left alone, like an art or drama teacher, and I would be able to use my status as a baseball coach to create a worthwhile experience that would not be afforded a new teacher. Below, I explored some of the moments we had as a group.

How would I be able to see some progress? I thought, "Maybe journals," "no, a film, we had technology in school." What was my reality? I was just trying to deal with that question, about race and equality, and opening up conversations through the use of slavery paradigms would lead to learning beyond or in spite of me for the students. Elliot Eisner (1979/1985) emphasizes that time is crucial to change. Sometimes programs are not given a chance to prove themselves. Ideas have to be given a chance to cause change: "they are historical and transitory products" (Shapiro, 1980, p. 159). Ideas are dynamic; some catch on quickly and cause immediate change, while others take time and cause change over time. For example, many of the Civil Rights reformers had been educated after World War II, when they were taught that the war was fought to end the racist and fascist regime of Germany. The lessons they learned in school took almost twenty years to manifest themselves.

A target of the curriculum was for the learners to be critical of themselves, and that as individuals they shape the world around them. A beginning point would be the passive resistance paradigm, which allows the individual to seek questions they could not otherwise. In seeing slavery from the point of view of passive resistors, people who consciously resisted through nonrevolutionary means, opens possibilities for creating space for change on a personal level. When we ask questions of resistance, we can discover ourselves and connect to the acts we see in slave narratives. Learners must be given opportunities to ask questions of passive resistance. These questions can be brought by introducing the model of slavery, concentrating on the slaves as free-thinking individuals who chose passive resistance over overt revolt. The person had to operate within an oppressive society and its boundaries, which included death for violating rules. Even though many of my students were familiar with death, either from stories of immigration from Haiti or from the violent crime in their neighborhood, their everyday actions would not cause death. They lived in a violent world, but the safety of the space I could provide would hopefully allow them to question through passive resistance, beginning a journey toward the question of conflict between freedom and racism. How could the paradigm be applied in the classroom? What could I do to create an atmosphere that allowed spaces for such questions and let students make choices in such questions, specifically since many would be in place that required banked information in social studies influencing their graduation? In hindsight, I admit that I was not too worried because I knew many would not pass writing and math, so the point was moot. In my own way, I was trying to encourage critical reading and writing to help them, while at the same time worrying about not teaching the curriculum. The freedom I possessed might harm the learners. That tumultuous dichotomy drove the quarter in U.S. history; their zest fueled my curriculum and their failure fueled my apprehensions.

In successful passive resistance, the slave recognized who they were and how far they could go in creating freedom spaces. Passive resistance is an active act of a critically thinking person. Schools must be active in relating what the possibilities in using passive resistance in a student's life, and its consequences. The connection must be made between the past (slavery) and the present (racial stratification) by the student as they ask themselves how the events they study and see from the past appear to look like today. What remnants are we living with today. Although each student's approach and definitions will be different, they will hopefully find common ground.

I name this curricular approach the theory and praxis problem-solving curriculum model. Self-evaluation of the curriculum would come from the Aptheker/Stampp resistance paradigm. In this paradigm the individual slaves felt freedom through passive resistance. They were able to regain their humanity through covert acts of defiance. For example, after reading several narratives, including Frederick Douglass, I asked my students for examples of passive resistance in their lives. Some examples the students offered were surprising. Lakeisha, the oldest of five and only sixteen, proudly said that "she lived a life of passive resistance." She continued, "Not doing a chore gets me recognition for how important I am to the house." Of course, she felt more power in explaining why she missed out on the task than in the action. "My momma just doesn't get this passive resistance." After several oral and written exercises to elicit responses, I began to see students distinguishing between "breaking a rule," and actually using passive resistance. For example, Sylvan never had books, except for Spanish and U.S. history. Delving into his reasoning, I discovered that in social studies and Spanish he felt a part of the class for many different reasons. He was "not very good at English," "cain't do no Math," but I like the other stuff. He said, "leaving books at home, I got Ms. Fischer and Coach Orlando to get me extra attention." I patted myself on the back for such a great conversation. It went on like that for a week, becoming more sophisticated each time. I prided myself on my ability to have a free and open classroom conducive to truthful dialogue like Freire's in *Pedagogy of the Oppressed*. Yet there were problems. Was I listening to only what I wanted to hear? Was this just an exercise in class? Would it have any effect beyond the experience? These questions of uncertainty are what should drive teaching, especially in social studies where interpretation is crucial in the retelling/re-creating of history for the learners. I also wondered if this was easier because of the students I was working with. Of the thirty-eight students, which thirty-four showed up regularly a feat since the school's average daily attendance was around 60%, twenty-four were Haitian immigrants and only ten of them were born in the United States. The other fourteen students were African American and second- and third-generation immigrants. Their lives and situation lent themselves to this type of approach. It took me years to realize that the improvised curriculum created was conducive to the learners. It was mere accident, and I could not explain why it was successful. Returning to the school years later and speaking to students currently attending, I saw that the difference might have been in creating a space that was not dominated by standardized curriculum, which I myself taught in the other sections of U.S. history and world history. This experiment was just for one class and would have never happened had JaSheena not asked her insightful question.

Next, I wanted to introduce the concepts of slavery and freedom as modern concepts. What did slavery and freedom mean to the students? They used the examples of school and home as limiting institutions that restrict their freedoms, and from which they could not run. I feared that my curriculum degraded slavery to rules set by parents and teachers. I thought the experiences we had earlier failed. At a loss for what to do, I called Joe, a local preacher who had led the integration of several schools in Miami. He lived in a tumultuous time in the 1960s and again was thrust into the spotlight when he helped calm down the Miami riots in 1989. He would surely shed light on the difference between resistance to oppression and parental rules. I also believed for the students those were rules they saw as oppressive and slave-like. I also asked my mother and many of her friends who spent ten years in a political prison in Cuba for questioning and fighting against what they believed was Fidel Castro's dictatorship. The stories from the Cuban women were very powerful, especially for the men in class, who never saw this power and defiance in women. Many found parallels to their grandmothers and mothers in raising and fighting for their families or in their lives in Haiti and decision to get on a boat and sail to Miami. Their examples of passive resistance did not live up to those of the guests. Many went home and began interviewing relatives who had faced oppression in Haiti or lived through the Civil Rights Movement. This was spontaneous and came from a suggestion. Elvis said that his sixth grade teacher made him interview his grandmother to find out about what it was like to live through the depression (he confessed that it was impossible since his grandmother was only forty at the time). That idea gave me an inroad on creating a place for connections between slavery and oppression. Many recognized passive resistance as liberating, because as Irving said "even in bondage we can still hold on to the concept of freedom." I asked where he learned that, and he said that he "got it from that Douglass (autobiography of Frederic K. Douglass) thing we read; he sounded a lot like Martin Luther King." Tonya asked me if they knew each other. The explanation on which both men were opened a world for historical learning. We have robbed history of its essence. In teaching things like "first history," we rob the learner of a sense of historical time.[1] In retelling why these men and others did not live concurrently, I embarked on a new journey with he class, an attack on social studies curriculum and its teaching of American history. An "attack upon the authoritative institutions in which custom and tradition are embodied is, therefore, as naturally resented by the individual; it is deeply resented as an attack upon what is deepest and truest in himself" (Ratner, 1939, p. 348). We rarely question the teaching of history as teachers, parents, or students in public schools. In the case of Miami, testing was driving the content of the course in the mid-1990s. For the students this represented a fear of failure that many had resided to just avoid. The only test that mattered for them was the High School Competency Test necessary for graduation. The rest were just not important. In fact, many had grown up in a world where testing in public education was foreign. The state of Florida only gave two tests, the Stanford Achievement Test in tenth grade and the High School Competency Test in eleventh grade. As Ivan Illich stated, this education through certification, learning was only justifiable through accountability to a superstructure in the state of Florida.

The important aspect of this lesson is not the questions from the process but that the theories and practices of each learner came into contact with those of the persons describing oppression in their lives. The autobiography project "challenge[d] educators to begin with the individual experience and then make broader connections" to their world (Slattery, 1995, p. 58). The autobiographical connection to the broader society cannot be made without a larger perspective or goal, as described in the linear curriculum schools have adopted. For Dewey the connection occurred when the school allowed the learner self-recognition and a space for connection to society. How to connect the freedom of learning with a society obsessed with accountability through quantity and certification in public education proved a difficult task. Alienation of the individual occurred, and the nature of critical thought I thought could only be reached through autobiographical curriculum. I believed that involved a sense of connection, what Pinar means when he states that "we can no longer remain ahistorical, detached, impersonal, and behaviorally objective" (Slattery, 1995, p. 66). The watershed in living this idea evolves from the lack of independence when we remain attached to a linear set of curricula and institutions. The risk that a teacher runs by living out this curriculum is alienating the learner without agency in a structural functional institution. Thus, alienation is a real possibility. Ironically enough, it was an attempt at changing the curriculum focuses around learning that could end in individual alienation.

The second paradigm, the economic paradigm, advanced by Robert Fogel and Stanley Engerman is the best way to examine society. Fogel and Engerman's model is dehumanizing, because individuals serve a secondary purpose to the structure. This theory is derived from the work of Talcott Parsons (1937), who views individuals as having a place within the structure. Individuals must adapt to the structure, which changes if it needs to. Each person has a function. The teacher must relate slavery as an economic structure to the present-day context of the learner's life. This is the easiest model to relate to the learner. They will be able to find a plethora of examples that dehumanize them, such as tracking, test scores, the school system, Department of Motor Vehicles, the federal, state, and local governments. The teacher must teach the student that although society is technological, it is the job of the free and critical learner to humanize it (Smart, 1993). The learner can find attempts by the people she interviewed to deal with their dehumanizing situation. We use them to construct knowledge, build connections, and ultimately change the world.

The third step in personal liberation is addressed in the autobiographical paradigm. This paradigm allows the individual to form dyadic and other personal relationships within a dehumanizing paradigm. Small groups, unlike individuals, can cause significant change. For example, if one plantation mistress can teach a slave boy to read (Frederick Douglass) causing change in his life, imagine if a group of mistresses taught many boys to read, what would the change be? This action can lead to immense societal change: revolution. If this curriculum works, then blacks can realize that not all whites are racist, that they are practicing (racial stratification) because they do not realize that it is in conflict with their theory (freedom). Blacks can make them realize their conflict and thus begin a truthful dialogue. Also, if whites realize that conflict exists, then they can be truthful about what steps to take in order to fix the problem. Blacks can also realize that closing themselves in their past is harmful, that through truthful dialogue they can become active pursuers of their rightful share. Dialogue is our first step to acceptance. Words like love and respect will be able to regain their meaning. Language will once again be truthful; it will not hold double meaning.

Slattery states that "poststructural curriculum challenges students to enter history rather than simply observe history from a distance" (Slattery, 1995, p. 38). This statement is what Dewey had in mind in establishing the Chicago Laboratory School, or Counts in asking schools to change and the type of curriculum Ralph Tyler championed in the *Eight Year Study* (1932–1940). In poststructuralism, the learners must act as "participants rather than as observers" (Slattery, 1995, p. 39). Poststructuralists' problems rest not with the curriculum, but like Ivan Illich (1971), their conflict is with the institutionalization of learning. Respecting the individual's history as being true, which is what American schools have tried to do since the Civil Rights Movement, made us aware of our mistakes. Without freeing the critical individual, change can never take place. Respect cannot be achieved through decree or legislation; it can only occur through reeducation and dialogue (see Bene et al., 1971).

For Popper "criticism consists in the search for contradiction and in their elimination: the difficulty created by the demand for their elimination constitutes a new problem" (Popper, 1972, p. 126). The first step in social change is applying this set of questions to the new liberated student. Popper (1984/1992) states that solutions are open to criticism, and we must attempt to refute them, if the solution fails our criticism, we propose another, if it survives we "accept it worthy of further discussion and criticism" (p. 66). Thus, the newly liberated individual can begin to question society in search for the truth, once they find a solution; the liberated individuals must then attempt to change society.

References

Anderson, B. (1991). *Imagined Communities.* New York: Verso.
Apple, M. (1996). *Cultural Politics and Education.* New York: Teachers College Press.
Aptheker, H. (1943/1989). *Abolitionism: A Revolutionary Movement.* Boston, MA: Twayne Publishers.
Benne, K., Bennis, W. and Chin, P. (1971). *The Planning of Change.* New York: Holt/Rinehart.
Berger, P., and Luchmann, T. (1967). *The Social Construction of Reality.* New York: Anchor.
Brantlinger, E. (2004). *Dividing Classes.* New York: Routledge.
Breen, T. H. (1980). *Myne Owne Ground: Race and Freedom on Virginia's Eastern Shore, 1640–1676.* New York: Oxford University Press.
Burns, J. M. (1978). *Leadership.* New York: Harper and Row.
Castanell, L. & Pinar, W. (1993). *Curriculum as Racial Text.* Albany, NY: SUNY Press.
Counts, G. S. (1932). *Dare the Schools Build a New Social Order?* New York: John Day Co.
———. (1971). *The American Road to Culture.* New York: Arno Press.
Culler, J. (1976/1979). *Structuralist Poetics: Structuralism, Linguistics, and the Study of Literature.* Ithaca, NY: Cornell University Press.
Derrida, J. (1978). *Writing and Difference.* Trans. A. Bass. Chicago: University of Chicago Press.
———. (1981). *Positions.* Chicago: University of Chicago Press.
———. (1982). *Margins of Philosophy.* Trans. A. Bass. Chicago: University of Chicago Press.
Donmoyer, R. (1991). The First Glamourizer of Thought: Theoretical and Autobiographical Ruminations on Drama and Education. In G. Willis and W. Schubert (Eds.), *Reflections from the Heart of Educational Inquiry.* Albany, NY: State University of New York Press, 73–91.
Eisner, E. (1979/1985). *The Educational Imagination: On the Design & Evaluation of School Programs.* New York: Macmillan College Publishing Company.
Fields, B. (1982). Ideology and Race in AMERICAN History. In J. M. Krousser and J. M. McPherson (Eds.), *Region, Race and Reconstruction: Essays in Honor of C. Vann Woodward* (pp. 283–313). New York: Routledge.
Fogel, R., and S. Engerman (1974). *Time on the Cross: The Economics of American Slavery.* Boston, MA: Harvard University Press.
Foucault, M. (1977). *Language, Counter-Memory, Practice: Selected Essays and Interviews.* Trans. and ed. D. Bouchard. Ithaca, NY: Cornell University Press.
———. (1980). *Power/Knowledge.* New York: Pantheon.
Fox-Genovese, E. (1988). *Women in the Plantation Household: Black and White Women of the Old South.* Chapel Hill, NC: University of North Carolina Press.
Fredrickson, G. M. (1982/1988) *The arrogance on race.* Middletown, CT: Wesleyan University Press.
Freire, P. (1970). *Pedagogy of the Oppressed.* New York: Continuum.
Genovese, E. (1974). *Roll, Jordan, Roll.* New York: Norton.
Giddens, D. (1976). *New Rules of Sociological Method.* London: Hutchinson.
———. (1991). *Modernity and Self-Identity.* Palo Alto, CA: Stanford University Press.
Giroux, H. (1988). *Teachers as Intellectuals.* Westport, CT: Bergin and Garvey.

Habermas, J. (1992). *Postmetaphysical Thinking: Philosophical Essays.* Trans. W. Hohengarten. Cambridge, MA: The MIT Press.

Illich, I. (1971). *Deschooling Society.* New York: Harper & Row.

Lyotard, J. F. (1984). *Condition Postmodernne.* Trans. G. Bennington. Minneapolis, MN: University of Minnesota Press.

Morgan, E. (1975). *American Slavery, American Freedom: The Ordeal of Colonial Virginia.* New York: Norton.

Onuf, N. (1989). *World of Our Making.* Columbia, SC: University of South Carolina Press.

Parsons, T. (1937). *Structure of Social Action.* New York: McGraw Hill.

Pinkard, T. (1994). *Hegel's Phenomenology: The Sociality of Creation.* New York: Cambridge University Press.

Popper, K. (1972). *Objective Knowledge: An Evolutionary Approach.* London: Oxford University Press.

———. (1984/1992). *In Search of a Better World: Lectures and Essays from Thirty Years.* New York: Routledge.

Ratner, J. (1939). *Intelligence in the Modern World: John Dewey's Philosophy.* New York: Modern Library.

Rorty, R. (1979). *Philosophy and the Mirror of Nature.* Princeton, NJ: Princeton University Press.

———. (1982). *Consequences of Pragmatism.* Minneapolis, MN: University of Minnesota Press.

Shapiro, L. (1980). The Concept of Ideology as Evolved by Marx and Adapted by Lenin. In M. Cranston, P. Mair, and M. Nijhoff (Eds.), *Ideology and Politics.* The Hague: Kluer Academic Publishing.

Slattery, P. (1995). *Curriculum Development in the Postmodern Era.* New York: Garland Publishing.

Smart, B. (1993). *Postmodernism.* New York: Routledge

Stampp, K. (1956). *The Peculiar Institution.* New York: Routledge.

Tyler, R. W. (1949). *Basic Principles of Curriculum.* Chicago: University of Chicago Press.

Williams, E. (1964/1966). *Capitalism and Slavery.* London: Andre Deutch.

9

Flags and Homeschooling

Symbols of Freedom and Democracy

JENNIFER DEETS

In 1988, I spent the fall semester of my undergraduate senior year at the Pushkin Institute in Moscow, when it was still the Union of Soviet Socialist Republics. In October our group took an excursion to the city of Tblisi in Soviet Georgia. The week following our return, the beautiful city and its inhabitants were devastated by a massive earthquake. The nation responded with a two-week mourning period during which the familiar red flag with its hammer and sickle was modified by black stripes affixed along the bottom edge or with black bows tied atop the poles. These omnipresent black-tipped flags were potent symbols of shared grief.

Toward the end of my four-month stay in the Soviet Union another flag captured my imagination. This time it was the flag of the United States. After weeks and weeks of steadfastly avoiding anything American, I ended up on a walk that took me right past the United States Embassy. When I saw the flag flying, I remember thinking, "Now that's a real flag!" I was instantly dismayed by the ethnocentricity of my response, but it dramatically heightened my awareness of the importance and power of symbols.

As a patriotic gesture following the terrorist attacks of September 11, 2001, a student group at the public university where I taught donated flags to be displayed in every classroom on campus. A group of faculty members and students objected to the flags and circulated a petition asking the university president to return the gift. A fellow department member, a Canadian, attempted to garner my support.

I told him that I had fought for that flag as a symbol of his right, even as a guest in my country, to state his objections openly without fear of harm. I would not oppose the flag's display anywhere.

Those three lessons have remained with me and help me to recognize homeschooling as a flag of freedom and democracy in the United States. FDR said in his speech on January 6, 1941, "Since the beginning of our American history we have been engaged in change—in a perpetual peaceful revolution—a revolution which goes on steadily, quietly adjusting itself to changing conditions . . ." Homeschooling is part of that peaceful revolution by being a strong, successful counterpoint to a strong, successful educational system, offering a different perspective on freedom and democracy for a future filled with unimagined challenges and opportunities, a future that requires the people of this country to be as well equipped as possible to endure as well as enjoy what is to come.

Homeschooling

In order to examine homeschooling as a symbol for freedom and democracy in the U.S., it must be situated in time and must be clearly defined. Although homeschooling is the oldest form of education in the world as families from the dawn of time have taken care to rear their children with skills necessary to physically survive and to socially thrive wherever they have lived, homeschooling today is something distinctly different. As it is understood in contemporary society, homeschooling is more than adults teaching children outside of institutional schools; it is a social and political undertaking and can only exist in one of two scenarios: openly in contrast to a flourishing public, democratic educational system or secretly in an oppressive state where the educational system is in any way discriminatory.

Homeschooling as a movement began in the 1960s although varieties of it existed well before the twentieth century (O'Connell, 1998). One need only remember the prohibition of education for slaves and for girls to recognize that the subversive variety of homeschooling had ample room to grow. With stringent truancy laws, families who objected to compulsory education for their children had to conduct their studies in secret, keeping the children out of sight until after school hours. As parents fought the state to regain control over their right to rear—including the right to educate—their own children, and as their children revealed no ill effects of being educated at home, laws were modified. With year after year of success, including widely published accomplishments of homeschooled children, the climate has become, if not welcoming, at least less hostile to homeschoolers.

Homeschooling exists on a continuum from a replication of school at home replete with bells, desks, and worksheets, to a loosely structured set of educational experiences embedded in everyday life called unschooling. Homeschooling families traditionally looked to themselves and local resources for educational materials, but with the advent of distance education programs for school-age children, families can travel, serve as volunteers anywhere in the world, or simply create a more flexible family life by subscribing to one of the available programs. Although many of the families who use such programs call themselves homeschoolers, some simply provide the materials to their children, leaving the instruction to the media and instructors located at other sites. Similarly, many families who have a homeschooling ethos—trying to find the learning potential in any experience—find that they must by necessity enroll their children in local schools. These two situations reveal the challenges inherent in determining the extent of homeschooling in the United States.

In states where homeschooling is permitted, homeschoolers must voluntarily register their children as homeschoolers. In other states, homeschoolers must set up small private schools and report that their children are enrolled in the schools. In all states some families still resist reporting anything to a state agency and who, in effect, homeschool underground as did almost all of the early homeschoolers. Thus, when the bureau of educational statistics reports that, as of 2001, 850,000 children are registered homeschoolers, that figure must be recognized as on the very low end of accurate (Lines, 1999). Most homeschooling researchers estimate the number to be at least twice as many if not more (Ray, 1997).

One of the significant challenges of early homeschooling was that children, often highly motivated, clever, and capable, were unable to document their courses of study and could not gain admission to colleges and universities for advanced coursework. Certainly exceptions have always existed, but only in the past ten years has it become common for homeschooled children to have equitable chances at admission as traditionally schooled children. While college education itself may be valuable, in contemporary society, the college credential is crucial for certain kinds of advancement and success. Obtaining access to that credential was essential for the movement to continue to thrive and grow.

Homeschooling and FDR's Four Freedoms

Using homeschooling as a way to examine the "four essential human freedoms" outlined by FDR in his January 6, 1941, speech, I hope to illustrate how homeschooling sheds light on what freedom and democracy mean in the United States. The premise of FDR's speech was that "at no previous time has American security been as seriously threatened from without as it is today." Such a sentiment has lain over the American psyche since the terrorist attacks of September 11, 2001. Although four years have passed and action as dramatic as war has been taken to fight the real and imagined perils of terrorist aggression, a raw vulnerability remains exposed in the American hide. No longer the invincible wild west of lore, contemporary America struggles to maintain its integrity with its founding ideals as well as its historical courses of action tempered with a new reality that could not have been anticipated. Such a struggle demands a clear understanding of who we Americans have been, how we have acted, and why, and thus an examination of FDR's moving speech and his assertion that there exist four essential human freedoms is a worthwhile endeavor.

Freedom of Every Person to Worship God in His Own Way

I begin with this freedom because of two widespread misconceptions. One misconception is that homeschoolers are almost universally religious, in particular, Christians with fundamentalist beliefs. Another misconception is that they homeschool because of those beliefs. In fact, although many homeschoolers are practicing Christians, their faith is not always why they choose to homeschool. Reasons for homeschooling vary widely (e.g., Gray, 1992; Harrison, 1996; Hetzel, 1998; Rudner, 1999; Welner & Welner, 1999).

Some families homeschool because they believe they can provide academic experiences that surpass what are offered in schools. A subset of these families has children with special needs who are either vastly above or significantly below the norms, and therefore in need of specialized instruction, instruction that is ostensibly provided in schools, but may not be what the families desire or believe to be most appropriate for their children.

Other families choose homeschooling because they are concerned about the social environment of increasingly large, centralized, and potentially impersonal schools. Even if all else is suitable about their local schools, some families simply want to ease their children from childhood to adulthood with social environments that involve interaction with children and adults of all age groups, not simply agemates from year to year.

Still other families choose to homeschool because they want their children to have unstructured time for learning and growth. These families typically have few academic routines and their children learn material at different rates and in different order than schooled children do. It is not unusual to find one of these unschooled children beginning physics at age 10 through an apprenticeship with a neighborhood research scientist or for another to concentrate on turtles, studying them with an intensity typically observed only with graduate students, using that focus to expand into other academic areas like geography, literature, and science.

Some families homeschool because they travel too frequently to warrant enrolling their children in school after school or because they live in remote areas for extended periods of time while the parents conduct research or provide services to communities throughout the world.

Still, for some families, it *is* a commitment to a religious ideal that drives them to take on the responsibility of educating their children at home. The "freedom of every person to worship God in his own way" provides for this choice in a society that prides itself on its egalitarian educational offerings. Where families glorify their God and live out their understanding of His directives by homeschooling their children, they reveal the vitality of this freedom.

Freedom of Speech and Expression

In a country where some people have until all-too-recently been excluded from educational opportunities that permit social and economic advancement, homeschoolers are often regarded as unappreciative of what is available to them. At best, they are regarded as elitist for their abandonment of the system. Their children are expected to succeed wildly because, after all, who wouldn't succeed after being privately tutored for so many years?

At worst, homeschoolers are regarded with suspicion because of the sentiment that reasonable parents would not withhold the mainstream school experience from their children (Lyster-Mensh, 2001). To do so would be to set the children up as social misfits, forever unable to relate to their schooled peers. The occasional horrifying tragedy of a family using homeschooling as an excuse to harm the children does not diminish this perception at all nor does it reassure concerned individuals who regard school as a way to ensure the physical safety of children.

Yet these are not realistic perceptions. Most research that deals with homeschooling focuses on the academic success of homeschoolers (e.g., Moss, 1995; Ray, 1997). What little research deals with the social lives of homeschooled children reveals them to be well-adjusted, happy, socially capable children and equally socially adept adults (Schemmer, 1985; Schellenberger, 1998). Moreover, attending school does not eradicate the incidence of abuse of children any more than homeschooling increases its likelihood.

That stereotypes exist about homeschooling, that homeschooling continues to thrive, and that multiple points of view can be heard are indicators of a healthy freedom of speech and expression in this country.

Freedom from Fear

Roosevelt meant for this freedom to be a freedom from the fear of armed conflict. Although choices about how a family will ensure that their children are educated are not exactly armed conflict, the road to the current acceptance of homeschooling has not been smooth. From the beginning of the common school in the United States, governing bodies have struggled with how to define who can and who must go to school.

When families wanted to *not* send their children to school, the children were considered truant and the parents, irresponsible. Such a hostile environment forced many families into underground homeschooling, willing to choose what they believed to be best for their children over the existing rules regarding compulsory attendance. These families resisted the notion that the state knew better what the greater good was for their children.

These staunch early homeschoolers defied both society and the law in order to effect change in a system that was too oppressive for them. Since those early days, and with the continuing efforts of homeschoolers throughout the country, laws have been changed and provisions made for both the welfare of the greatest number of children in the country as well as the rights of families to rear their children as they deem appropriate.

While freedom of speech and expression and freedom to worship God sound wonderful, without a freedom from fear, those rights cannot be fully exercised. The early homeschooling families' actions contributed greatly to a reduction in fear and made it possible for homeschooling to grow in popularity.

While the homeschooling movement openly challenges the schooling system, it also provides opportunities to highlight strengths and disadvantages of both, ironically, drawing them closer together through distance education and comprehensive, detailed curriculum packages virtually identical to those used in schools. From hostility to ambivalence to acceptance, homeschooling also represents a freedom from fear in the educational system, revealing it to be flexible enough for the vast majority of school-age children, but tolerant enough to accept that it cannot meet every need or desire of every family in the United States. Homeschooling therefore represents a freedom from fear for individual families as well as a freedom from fear for an establishment, both essential in the creation of the best education possible for all children in the country.

Freedom from Want

Early homeschoolers often chose to homeschool because the local schools did not provide what they sought for their children. They had wants and needs that were not being met. They also had fear that they would be arrested and, potentially, their children taken away, for their well-intentioned defiance of the laws of the time.

However, not all homeschooling families choose homeschooling in opposition to school. Some choose to educate their children *for* the benefit of the family. For them, homeschooling is not an act of resistance; it is a commitment to potential, to hope, and to possibility. While these families realize that homeschooling implies a rejection of the educational system that currently exists, their commitment to family, their children, and their goals for academic growth demand that they homeschool. In these cases, homeschooling represents reclamation of the joy and beauty in learning and teaching. It is a positive expression of an unmet need or want.

Most homeschoolers organize co-ops, help their youngsters participate authentically in their communities, and participate actively in local education and other institutions. They recognize that for each family a different set of circumstances, including expectations and abilities, drives what and how the children are educated. These families are concerned about the welfare and education of all children by whatever means necessary.

Expressed as an ability to choose and create something that was lacking before represents the manifestation of FDR's "freedom from want." Homeschooling is not an expression of freedom from economic want, but the ability to choose the educational path for one's children that addresses FDR's claim that freedom from want contributes to a "healthy peacetime life for its inhabitants."

Freedom and Flags

In a nation at war and with the specter of terrorism lingering in our national view, we can easily become cynical about freedom and democracy. Perhaps the lessons from homeschooling as an exemplar of FDR's four freedoms can provide insight into how the four freedoms can be obtained, as he emphatically desired, "everywhere in the world."

United States troops have been engaged in battles for three long years in Iraq and even longer in Afghanistan. They and the people who support democracy in those lands are certainly not enjoying freedom from fear. The local people are also painfully unable to enjoy freedom from want—economic or political. Until terrorists and insurgents are stopped, freedom of speech and expression are only an ideal. And in a world where religious teachings are manipulated to justify violence and oppression, freedom to worship God is also only a dream.

To people in these places, homeschooling might well be a beacon of hope, a flag of possibility. Where they maintain a spirit of courage and optimism, they likely are teaching young people about the ways things could be. These subversive, secret schools, some formal, some loosely organized, represent the incredible power of homeschooling. Where children continue to learn about their past and the future they can create, they inspire each other to stand firm and to persevere in their own peaceful revolution.

Their efforts as well can inspire us in the United Sates to appreciate anew that the four freedoms, although fraught with the potential for tension, nevertheless permit interaction and experience that make us all stronger, together.

References

Arai, A. B. (1999). Homeschooling and the redefinition of citizenship. *Education Policy Analysis Archives, 7*(27). [online] Available at http://epaa.asu.edu/epaa/v7n27/.

Broadhurst, D. (1999). *Investigating young children's perceptions of homeschooling.* Paper presented at the 1999 AARE Conference Melbourne Paper No. BRO99413 [CD-ROM] AARE WWW Easter 2000, ISSN 1324-9320. Melbourne: Australian Association for Research in Education.

Farber, P. J. (2001). The new face of homeschooling. *Harvard Education Letter (17),* 2, 1–4.

Gray, S. (1992). *Why some parents choose to homeschool.* Unpublished doctoral dissertation. University of California Los Angeles.

Grubb, D. (1998). *Homeschooling: Who and why?* Paper presented at the Annual meeting of the Mid-South Educational Research Association, New Orleans, LA.

Gustavsen, G. (1981). *Selected characteristics of home schools and parents who operate them.* Unpublished doctoral dissertation, Andrews University.

Hanna, L. G. (1996). *Homeschooling in the 1990s: An issue of access.* Unpublished doctoral dissertation, Immaculaa College.

Harrison, S. M. (1996). *A qualitative study of motivational factors for choosing to homeschool: Experiences, thoughts, and feelings of parents.* Unpublished doctoral dissertation, Gonzaga University.

Hegener, M., & Hegener, H. (Eds.). (1988). *The home school reader.* Tonasket, WA: Home Education Press.

Hetzel, D. J. (1998). *Factors that influence parents to homeschool.* Unpublished doctoral dissertation, The Claremont Graduate University, Claremont, CA.

Knowles, J. G. (1988). Introduction: The context of home schooling. *Education and Urban Society (21),* 5–15.

———. (1991). Parents' rationales for operating home schools. *Journal of Contemporary Ethnography 20* (2), 203–231.

Lande, N. (1996). *Homeschooling: A patchwork of days.* Bozeman, MT: WindyCreek.

Lange, C. M., & Liu, K. K. (1999). *Homeschooling: Parents' reasons for transfer and the implications for educational policy.* Minneapolis: National Center on Educational Outcomes.

Leue, M. M. (Ed.). (1994). *Challenging the giant: The best of Skole, the journal of alternative education.* (Vol. 2). Albany, NY: Down-to Earth Books.

Lines, P. M. (1999). Homeschoolers: Estimating numbers and growth. Washington, DC: US Dept. of Education, OERI. [online] Available http://www.ed.gov/offices/OERI/SAI/homeschool

Lyster-Mensh, L. (2001). "Not that it's any of my business, but . . .":Dealing with criticism of your decision to homeschool. National Home Education Network. [online] Available http://www.nhen.org/nhen/pov/newhser/not_any_business.html

Martin, M. (1997). *Homeschooling: Parents' reactions*. In *Perspectives in Education and Deafness*, (v 17, n.2. p 15).
Mayberry, M. (1988). Characteristics and attitudes of families who homeschool. *Education and Urban Society 21*, 32–41.
Meehan, N., & Stephenson, S. (1994). *Homeschooling in the United States: A review of recent literature*. Loyola College in Maryland.
Moss, P. A. (1995). *Benedictines without monasteries: Homeschoolers and the contradictions of community*. Unpublished doctoral dissertation, Cornell University, Ithaca, NY.
O'Connell, M. B. (1998). *Homeschooling: An historical inquiry*. Unpublished doctoral dissertation, University of Sarasota, Sarasota, FL.
Riley, D. (1994). *The Dan Riley school for a girl: An adventure in home schooling*. Boston: Houghton Mifflin.
Ray, B. (1997). *Strengths of their own: Academic achievement, family characteristics, and longitudinal traits*. Salem, OR: National Home Education Research Institute.
Rose, A. B. (1985). *A qualitative study of the characteristics of home schooling families in South Carolina and the perceptions of school district personnel toward home schooling*. Unpublished doctoral dissertation, University of South Carolina.
Rudner, L. M. (1999). Scholastic achievement and demographic characteristics of home school students in 1998. *Education Policy Analysis Archives, 7*(8). [online] Available at http://epaa.asu.edu/epaa/v7n8/.
Schellenberger, E. C. (1998). *An ethnographic case study of three homeschooling families in central Pennsylvania and their sociocultural support groups*. Unpublished doctoral dissertation, The Pennsylvania State University, State College.
Schemmer, B. A. S. (1985). *Case studies of four families engaged in home education*. Unpublished doctoral dissertation, Ball State University, Muncie, IN.
Van Galen, J. (1987). Explaining home education: Parents' accounts of their decisions to teach their own children. *The Urban Review (19)*, 3, 161–177.
———. (1988). Ideology, curriculum, and pedagogy in home education. *Education and Urban Society (21)*, 1, 52–68.
Watkins, M. A. C. (1997). *Are there significant differences in academic achievement between home-schooled and conventionally schooled students?* Unpublished master's thesis, University of Alberta.
Welner, K. M., & Welner, K. G. (1999). Contextualizing homeschooling data: A response. *Education Policy Analysis Archives, 7*(13). [online] Available at http://epaa.asu.edu/epaa/v7n13/.
Williamson, K. B. (1989). *Home schooling: Answering questions*. Springfield, IL: Charles C. Thomas.
Wolfe, R. J. (1997). Cultural meanings of homeschooling in the San Juan Islands of Washington State. Unpublished doctoral dissertation, Gonzaga University.

10
Democratizing Education
Lessons from the African American Experience

DONN C. WORGS AND LEON D. CALDWELL

In the years immediately following the Civil War, African Americans (most of whom had been enslaved) and their allies engaged in an extraordinary mobilization of resources and people aimed at bringing basic education to the black masses. Communities pooled their limited resources to build schools and support teachers. Where no schools existed, adults and children attended "classes" in a variety of locations—churches, homes, and in one Virginia city under a tree that came to be known as "Emancipation Oak" (Worgs, 2005). In the words of the renowned black educator and leader Booker T. Washington, "it was a whole race trying to go to school" (Washington, 1901, p. 30).

Why were they so obsessed with education? As historians have noted, the reasons behind these efforts were simple yet profound, both philosophical and practical. Blacks had been prohibited from learning during enslavement and came to equate ignorance with slavery. So the acquisition of knowledge and literacy were steps toward liberation. Many argued that if they were to remain free, they needed to be educated (Anderson, 1988). And of course there was the practical need to be able to read labor contracts and ballots (Worgs, 2005).

Thus, for African Americans in the nineteenth century, education was intimately connected to democracy and democratic possibilities. They sought education as a means to political empowerment—in both theoretical and practical ways. They understood the limits and the fragility of their "freedom," and they understood that the key to protection of rights and liberties was their own political participation. The extent to which they could determine their own destinies rested on their active democratic participation.

The story of African Americans during Reconstruction is one example of the interconnection between education and democracy in the United States. This is a relationship that has become even stronger since the nineteenth century. Formal public education (even private education to an extent as in the case of vouchers and charter schools) is shaped by the political process, and formal educational institutions are widely expected to prepare Americans for democratic citizenship.

Given the significance of this relationship, it is important to consciously craft practices and institutions to support the highest objectives related to democracy and education. The product of education in a democracy should be individuals prepared to fulfill their economic and cultural potential and also possess the knowledge, skills, and attitudes that support active political involvement. Falling short of this undermines the vitality of the American democracy.

Our primary contention follows John Dewey's claim that "democratic ends demand democratic means" (Dewey, 2001, p. 167). If American education is to produce the outcomes necessary for a thriving democracy, then that education itself must be "democratized." By this we mean that the education systems must promote and reflect the values of participatory democracy.

Democracy Clarified

Before further elaborating on the notion of democratizing education, it is important to clarify what we mean by the term "democracy" and our conceptions of democratic citizenship. This is critical, for as political scientist Robert Dahl noted, there is no one theory of democracy, there are "theories" of democracy (Terchek and Conte, 2001; Dahl, 1965). Moreover, differing conceptions of democratic citizenship carry significantly different educational implications, and ultimately significantly different political consequences (Westheimer and Kahne, 2004).

We advocate a vision of a participatory democracy that emphasizes inclusion and equality and respects and protects individual rights and liberties. This vision is not a radical departure from most popular understandings, yet we think it is important to highlight the notion of participatory democracy. Much discussion about the contemporary state of American democracy surrounds the need to protect liberties and rights. Though such discussions are extremely important, the discourse may ignore a critical component of American democracy—the responsibilities of participation and self-governance.

Although the notion of self-governance is at the core of the democratic idea, Americans seem too often to think of this self-governance as only a right, which it is, but not necessarily as a requirement. There is too little acknowledgment of the responsibility of governing. Consider, for example, the extent of citizen disengagement from education at the school district level. Whether, considering parent involvement, PTA membership, attendance at school board meetings, or participation in school board elections, few citizens are actively engaged in the governance of their public schools (National Center for Education Statistics, 1996; Putnum, 2000; Townley and Sweeney, 1994; Stone et al., 2001).

Any discussion of democracy and education needs to keep the notion of self-governance central. Without an understanding of the requirement of self-governance, democracy becomes something to be consumed rather than produced. The vitality of a democracy requires active participation, not passive expectations of rights, liberties, or fair representation by elected officials. African Americans in the post–Civil War South understood this, and hence used every available resource to access an education that would facilitate their active political participation. Our call for democratizing education is a call for greater citizen engagement in the shaping and delivery of education—particularly public elementary and secondary education (Caldwell, 2001). Unfortunately, a consideration of education practices, past and present, reveals that the shortcomings of American democracy have been undermining the education of Americans for quite some time.

Democracy and Education in Historical Context

Throughout American history, education and democracy have been intertwined. American education is a product of American democracy manifested through policies. Unfortunately, for much of American history, the project of educating citizens (and noncitizens) has too often been conducted in an undemocratic context: by undemocratic institutions, driven by undemocratic goals, using undemocratic methods. Consider the common school movement led by Horace Mann. As important as it was in terms of laying a foundation for later democratic developments in public education, this movement was rife with (un)democratic contradictions. Common school proponents sought to educate, and thus in a sense expand opportunities for effective citizenship, but they also sought to indoctrinate and to control, and thus their efforts ran counter to the freedoms and liberties supposedly revered (Kaestle, 1983; Spring, 2004).

The history of Native American education is another example. Through the nineteenth and much of the twentieth centuries, the stated goal of deculturalization—captured most succinctly by the phrase "kill the Indian and save the man"—was clearly not consistent with the principles of a liberal democracy (Worgs, 2000). Moreover, the oppressive educational experiences of both Mexican Americans and

Asian Americans further reveal the extent to which American educational practices veered from propounded principles (Spring, 2001).

Ultimately, education practices have really just been a reflection of the shortcomings of American democracy. Nothing illustrates this more than the experiences of African Americans. Not only was it illegal for enslaved Africans to learn to read, for much of the period of legalized enslavement, it was illegal for free African Americans as well. After emancipation and Reconstruction, state governments of the South were content to provide as little resources as possible for public education for blacks (Worgs, 2000; Anderson, 1988). But, as mentioned at the outset, the story is not solely one of oppression and sorrow. African American educational experiences reveal how democracy and education can be positively related when political activism is set to a movement.

Some of the most important moments in the evolution of American democracy came in relation to black education. For example, the era of legalized segregation was oppressive and quite undemocratic, but challenges to the system, in particular the education policies and practices, demonstrate the potential of the democratic impulse. The effort that supported the suit brought in *Brown v. Board of Education* is the best known, but the success of that case did not by itself transform segregated school systems. Desegregation, to the extent it was achieved, came as a result of mobilizations in Little Rock, New Orleans, Tuskegee, Prince Edward County, and Virginia where public schools were closed for over five years, and countless other localities throughout the South and eventually the North (Kirk, 2002; Morton, 1969; Norrell, 1985; Turner, 2003, 2004).

Interestingly, the battle to desegregate schools at times served as a catalyst for seizing political power and attaining political influence. This was the case in Cleveland where the effort of blacks and their allies to transform a segregated school system evolved into a movement that would result in the election of the nation's first black mayor of a major city (Moore, 2002). In all, although American democracy, as it was manifested through policies, was a detriment to black education, the democratic impulse within the people expanded educational opportunities and ultimately made the nation more democratic.

Overall, throughout the twentieth century, African Americans struggled for education resources, but were often constrained by the realities of an undemocratic politics. Their exclusion from government and the governance of public schools resulted in resource disparities as well as curricula that were often racist, and usually ethnocentric. The century of struggle, however, increased their political influence and brought reform—modest integration and reduced resource disparities. In terms of educational content, greater inclusion and participation has made a significant difference. Throughout the period of complete exclusion, there were challenges with regard to curricula—whether it was the debates about industrial or vocational education, tracking and special education, or, more recently, debates about racist or Euro-centric curricula. The emergence of multiculturalism, to an extent, provided a lexicon of inclusion and diversity that is now fairly widespread.

Democracy and Education in a Contemporary Context

Democracy and education continue to be intertwined. Though there is much to be proud of in terms of educational achievement—widespread literacy, the highest rates of high school and college graduation in U.S. history (U.S. Census Bureau, 2005)—the nation continues to underachieve relative to its potential to educate its people. We know today that segregation remains (Frankenberg et al., 2003), resource disparities and achievement gaps persist, and educators are still wrestling with what is the most appropriate curriculum for African American youth. Scholars have noted that curricular issues go beyond concerns about achievement disparities. For example, Caldwell (2002) suggested that African American student apathy was a by-product of cultural discontinuity as a result of monoethnic education that neglected to provide an accurate historical context of struggle for nonwhites. Ultimately, students left underprepared academically, alienated, and disengaged are inconsistent with the needs of democracy.

With widespread acknowledgment of the nation's educational shortcomings, why do these shortcomings persist? Scholars have offered a variety of theories and explanations for the nation's educational deficiencies. Since this discussion is centered on democracy and education, we focus on how democratic failings—failures within the political process—bear significant blame for the persistence of these shortcomings. Several scholars have shown that a lack of progress is due to the functioning of a political system that undermines progressive reforms, particularly at the local level (e.g., Anyon, 1997; Stone, 1998; Henig et al., 1999). At the federal level, it seems to us that the No Child Left Behind Act is illustrative of a policy shaped with limited input from communities and frontline educators—and subsequently its provisions are disconnected from the real needs of educators.

Though the chroniclers of the status quo often paint a rather dim picture of the possibilities of reform, we believe there are potent possibilities for change. Localities can transform their school systems and make tremendous educational progress provided they have the "civic capacity." According to Stone, "Civic capacity refers to the mobilization of varied stakeholders in support of a community-wide cause. Two elements enter into the picture. One is participation or involvement.... The other element is understanding" (Stone, 1998, p. 15). Reform possibilities lie in the capacity of communities to mobilize a variety of actors to engage in the process of reform. This is participatory democracy. At the root of civic capacity is an engaged citizenry. The extent to which political systems fail to make educational progress is in part a reflection of the disengagement of the citizens, as well as the resistance of elected officials and school administrators to allow democratic participation.

It is important to note, however, that this is not a one-way problem—politics undermining education. It may be more of a circular process, where politics hampers education and education hampers democratic politics. By many accounts, formal systems of education are doing a poor job of preparing students to actively engage in what is supposed to be a democratic society. It is a familiar story—young people are not developing the skills and attitudes necessary for democratic engagement. The evidence is familiar as well. Half of those eligible do not vote in presidential elections, and most eligible voters do not vote in mid-term state and local elections. And voting is the good news! Social scientists have been claiming for years that "civic engagement" is steadily declining, sparking debates about the need for civic education in elementary, secondary and postsecondary levels (Putnam, 2000; Colby et al., 2003; Quigley, 2004).

The Challenge: Democratizing Education

In a context in which the political process seems to have failed to consistently generate policies that generate educational outcomes consistent with the nation's potential, and educational systems seem to have a minimal impact in terms of preparing students for participatory democratic citizenship, the picture may seem bleak. Yet as the African American experience has shown, there is a latent democratic impulse within communities across the United States. Once this impulse is unleashed, the potential for democratic reform cannot be overstated.

Take, for example, the 2004 presidential election campaign and the hip-hop music driven voter mobilization efforts. The "Vote or Die" campaign led by hip-hop mogul Sean Combs in tandem with a series of "hip-hop Summits" organized by Russell Simmons were responsible for registering thousands of voters across the United States (Vargas, 2004; Hip-Hop Summit Action Network, 2005). Despite the negative images of rappers and hip-hop culture in the mainstream media, these efforts successfully mobilized legions of marginalized citizens, who tend to be the least likely to participate in politics. It is not clear to what extent these efforts, along with MTV's Rock the Vote campaign, were able to mobilize youth to actually vote, but it is clear that they registered thousands of voters, and postelection data indicated that the turnout of young people (18–24 years old) who voted was the highest in years (Center for Information and Research on Civic Learning and Engagement, 2005).

There is a latent democratic energy that only needs to be aroused. Consider the charter school movement, which, though controversial for a variety of reasons, has at times provided opportunities for expression of this democratic zeal. The formation of some charter schools has served as catalysts for the mobilization of resources and people for the purpose of educating or supporting education. In some African American communities these efforts have consciously responded to the need for more culturally affirming content and pedagogy to enter educational systems (e.g., the Amistad Academy in New Haven and the Betty Shabazz International Charter school in Chicago) (Sager, 2005; Epps, 2002).

We believe the means for providing the education necessary for democracy begins with a commitment to certain key democratic principles. As stated at the outset, we support Dewey's contention that democratic ends require democratic means. Specifically, we start from a premise that there is a need for widespread citizen engagement in the project of educating students. There needs to be greater involvement in the shaping and delivery of education. This requires citizens to take on the responsibility to be engaged, as the schools and school systems consciously become more open and inclusive. Of course this is not new. There are various calls for community schools, greater parent involvement, school-community partnerships, school-business partnerships, and so on. These measures are about citizen engagement and democracy and such measures need to be thought of and discussed within a context of democratic principles and objectives.

A participatory democratic ethos calls for citizens to be engaged, to care about, and to participate in the shaping of education. But the best efforts of an engaged citizenry may be thwarted by school systems that continue to reject parent and community engagement. Educating for democracy requires that the school systems be democratic institutions where committed adults can collectively shape the educational experiences of the community's students.

Democratizing education also calls for greater participation in the delivery of education to the student. Again the African American experience is instructive. Setting aside questions of political will, in the contemporary context, too many public school systems are unable to provide for all the educational needs of their students. Fortunately, there is a long legacy of black communities pooling resources to provide supplementary educational opportunities. They have sought to step in where the state has fallen short. There are numerous examples across the United States of activists and volunteers sacrificing to tutor and teach students in inner-city communities. One example is Hampton, Virginia, where for years a local church has organized volunteers to run after-school and tutoring programs in a number of schools across the city, and in two black neighborhoods, community members mobilized to create community centers, run largely by volunteers who tutor and teach elementary and secondary students, that offer GED classes, computer training, and other educational experiences (Stone and Worgs, 2004).

The Hampton example offers some important lessons. Contrary to much of the thinking on civic engagement (Putnum, 2000), such examples demonstrate that there are a number of people who want to be engaged in civic life, and will do so if they are given an opportunity. Moreover, the latent resource of energetic, skilled, and committed individuals can be tapped to help meet some of the challenges facing public schools systems. These kinds of efforts also serve the function of providing students with role models for engaged citizenship.

Conclusion

American democracy as manifest through the policies produced by the political process has failed American education, and education as constituted has failed American democracy. Ultimately educating for democracy demands an understanding that democracy offers freedoms but requires citizens to participate in self-governance. An education that supports this vision of democracy must be based upon a foundation of inclusion. Barriers to participation have to be removed, and school-community partnerships must be promoted. Such an education must promote engagement among students, not mere "community service," but active democratic engagement that prepares students for their responsibilities of self-governance. Civics courses alone will not initiate activism. Teachers must be unleashed by administrators to tackle the issues that students, at levels, see around them and can contribute to the dialogue of resolution. In all, education systems must promote and reflect the values of participatory democracy.

Democratizing education is critical to the well-being of American democracy. While the hip-hop summits and mobilization efforts such as the "Vote or Die" campaign can be important in terms of mobilizing people to action, these strategies are difficult if not impossible to sustain. More importantly, they are an inadequate substitute for extensive education. They are a great start, but they cannot provide the substantive political knowledge and skills that enable citizens to not only use their vote wisely, but to effectively engage the political system between elections. Knowledge and skills are essential to effective political participation (Westheimer and Kahne, 2004). We encourage broadening lesson plans beyond descriptions of political systems to skills necessary to participate in political systems. For example, developing courses that study revolution and rebellion at the middle school level could teach how to systematically organize a movement. Another example would be in teaching a class of high school students how to organize and conduct a rally or peaceful demonstration about an issue they care passionately about. Ironically some of these skills are those that students use to organize parties and other social gatherings.

As the nation continues to hold elections with declining participation, as rights are eroding, and as disparities of all types persist, it seems impossible to disagree with a notion that the United States is a "democratic facade." There are the trappings of democracy, but not the substance. And yet there is hope. The black experience shows us that democratic advancements can be made, and that education has been central to much of what democratic progress has been made. To achieve the substantive reality of democracy, we need to democratize education. In fact, there needs to be a democratic revolution within education. Until then, the nation will continue to struggle to produce citizens who will support substantive democratic society.

References

Anderson, J. (1988). *The Education of Blacks in the South, 1860–1935*. Chapel Hill: University of North Carolina Press.

Anyon, J. (1997). *Ghetto Schooling*. New York: Teacher's College Press.

Caldwell, L. D. (2001). Education as Talent Development: Preparing African American Students for a New Millennium: The Greenhouse or the Flower Shop. Illinois Committee on Black Concerns in *Higher Education Journal*. Carbondale, IL: Southern Illinois University Carbondale.

———. (2002). Fear of a Black Beret: Black College Students from Activism to Apathy. In J. Conyers (Ed.), *Race and Cultural Relations*. Westport, CT: Greenwood.

Center for Information and Research on Civic Learning and Engagement. (2005). The Youth Vote 2004. Fact Sheet. [S1] [S2] http://www.civicyouth.org, accessed October 5, 2006.

Colby, A., Ehrlich, T., Beaumont, E., and Stephens, J. (2003). *Educating Citizens: Preparing America's Undergraduates for Lives of Moral and Civic Responsibility*. San Francisco, CA: Jossey Bass.

Dahl, R. (1965). *A Preface to Democratic Theory*. Chicago: University of Chicago Press

Dewey, J. (2001). Democratic Ends Need Democratic Methods for Their Realization. In R. Terchek and T. Conte (Eds.), *Theories of Democracy*. Lanham, MD: Rowman & Littlefield, Part II, Section D.

Epps, E. (2002). Race and School Desegregation: Contemporary Legal and Educational Issues. *Penn GCE Perspectives on Education* 1(1) http://www.urbanedjournal.org/archive/Issue%201/FeatureArticles/article0003.html, accessed October 6, 2006.

Frankenberg, E., Lee, C., and Orfield, G. (2003). *A Multiracial Society with Segregated Schools: Are We Losing the Dream?* Cambridge, MA: The Civil Rights Project Harvard University.

Henig, J., Hula, R., Orr, M., and Pedescleeaux, D. (1999). *The Color of School Reform: Race, Politics and the Challenge of Urban Education*. Princeton, NJ: Princeton University Press.

Hip-Hop Summit Action Network. (2005). "Program Strategy" Hip Hop Summit Action Network.Org. www.hsan.org, accessed September 6, 2005.[S3]

Kaestle, C. (1983). *Pillars of the Republic: Common Schools and American Society 1780–1860*. Toronto, Canada: Harper Collins.

Kirk, J. (2002). *Redefining the Color Line: Black Activism in Little Rock, Arkansas, 1940–1970.* Gainesville: University Press of Florida.

Moore, L. (2002). The School Desegregation Crisis of Cleveland, Ohio 1963–64: The Catalyst for Black Political Power in a Northern City. *Journal of Urban History* 28(2), 135–157.

Morton, I. (1969). *Politics and Reality in an American City: The New Orleans School Crisis of 1960.* New York: Center for Urban Education.

National Center for Education Statistics. (1996). *Parents and Schools: Partners in Student Learning.* Statistics in Brief, Washington, DC.

———. (2002). *Digest of Education Statistics.* Washington, DC. http://nces.ed.gov/programs/digest/d02/, accessed February 5, 2007.

Norrell, R. (1985/1998). *Reaping the Whirlwind: The Civil Rights Movement in Tuskegee.* Chapel Hill: University of North Carolina Press.

Putnam, R. (2000). *Bowling Alone.* New York: Touchstone.

Quigley, C. (2004). *The Status of Civic Education: Making the Case for a National Movement.* The Center for Civic Education. www.civiced.org, accessed September 8, 2005.

Sager, R. (2005). The Charter School Revolution. *City Journal.* http://www.cityjournal.org/html/152sndgs04.htm, accessed October 2, 2006.

Spring, J. (2001). *Deculturalization and the Struggle for Equality: A Brief History of the Education of Dominated Cultures in the United States.* New York: McGraw-Hill.

———. (2004). *The American School, 1640–2004.* New York: McGraw-Hill.

Stone, C. (Ed.). (1998). *Changing Urban Education.* Lawrence, KS: University Press of Kansas.

Stone, C., Henig, J., Jones, B., and Pierannunzi, C. (2001). *Building Civic Capacity: The Politics of Reforming Urban Schools.* Lawrence, KS: University Press of Kansas.

Stone, C., and Worgs, D. (2004). Community Building and a Human-Capital Agenda in Hampton, Virginia: A Case Analysis of the Policy Process in a Medium-Size City. George Washington Institute for Public Policy Working Paper Series Working Paper Number 12.

Terchek, R., and Conte, T. (2001). *Theories of Democracy.* Lanham, MD: Rowman & Littlefield.

Townley, A., and Sweeney, D. (1994). School Board Elections: A Study of Citizen Voting Patterns. *Urban Education* 29(1), 50–62.

Turner, K. M. (2003). "Getting It Straight": Southern Black School Patrons and the Struggle for Equal Education in the Pre- and Post-Civil Rights Eras. *The Journal of Negro Education* 72(2), 217–229.

———. (2004). Both Victors And Victims: Prince Edward County, Virginia, The NAACP, and Brown. *Virginia Law Review* 90, 1667–1691.

U.S. Census Bureau. (2005). Percent of People 25 Years and Over Who Have Completed High School or College, by Race, Hispanic Origin and Sex: Selected Years 1940–2004. Historical Tables. http://www.census.gov/population/socdemo/education/tabA-2.pdf, accessed August 15, 2005.

Vargas, J. (2004). Vote or Die? Well They Did Vote. *Washington Post*, November 9, 2004.

Washington, B. T. (1901). *Up from Slavery.* Garden City, NY: Doubleday Electronic Edition. University of North Carolina at Chapel Hill. http://docsouth.unc.edu/washington/washing.html, accessed August 1, 2005.

Westheimer, J., and Kahne, J. (2004). What Kind of Citizen? The Politics of Educating for

Democracy. *American Educational Research Journal* 41(2), 237–269.

Worgs, D. (2000). Politics, Economics and Culture in the Production of African American and Native American Education. Doctoral Dissertation, University of Maryland, College Park.

———. (2005). Food for Starved Minds: The Mobilization of African American Communities for the Provision of Education. In A. Swain (Ed.), *Education as Social Action: Knowledge, Identity and Power*. New York: Palgrave MacMillan, Chapter 2.

11

Language of the Curriculum

Memes of Practice

JUDITH J. SLATER

Language is really the foundation of society as it creates understandings and allows human beings to use words to attempt to control future events. While words never give complete information about anything, there is an attempt to use language to regard the word as truth that fuels political, social, and economic interchanges and to impose behavior and belief on everyone. This reliance on language to communicate ideas impacts understandings and perceptions of any field, but is particularly influential in the field of education as the words used to describe the field are fraught with mass beliefs and concomitant behaviors that are duplicated all over the country, making each school district and each classroom similar in curriculum and pedagogy.

Another function of language is that it serves a biological function as it transmits information for self-preservation, creates and expresses social cohesion, controls behavior, and spurs the imagination creating symbols of reality. Language is also often a tool of society as it fuels ritual, informs through scientific reports, is used to persuade others, sway politically, prejudice, manipulate emotions, infer based on incomplete information, and make judgments of the worth and merit of something.

Therefore, the semantic environment, the interactions of humans in the educational community, makes certain assumptions about language. While much of language is talking, speaking, listening, reading, and writing, it is also the product of inner conscious and unconscious thoughts and assumptions. Those assumptions may be based on false maps and biased understandings that do not prepare a person for community. They may also be at odds with the experiences that a person will have in the future environment that pits their personal cultural heritage against the reality of experience. These dualities are the basis for freedom "from" language rather than freedom "of" language, the basis of which will be explored in this essay.

Language as a Biological Entity

Last summer I went to a Rodin exhibit in Vancouver. Rodin, master sculptor and interpreter of reality, wrote: "There is nothing more beautiful than the absolute truth of real existence." "The sculptor must learn to reproduce the surface, which means all that vibrates on the surface, soul, love, passion, life." What remarkable language from someone who used a visual medium to represent his inner thoughts. But, every artist, whether in the visual arts, writers, filmmakers, tomb builders, flower arrangers, or those who design the latest technology, make this transformation of idea into reality either through the production of real objects or through the formation of sentences, words strung together that represent and communicate reflective thought.

In 1951 Susanne Langer wrote:

> Language is, without a doubt, the most momentous and at the same time the most mysterious product of the human mind. Between the clearest animal call of love or warning or anger, and a man's least, trivial word, there lies a whole day of Creation—or in modern phrase, a whole chapter of evolution. In language we have the free, accomplished use of symbolism, the record of articulate conceptual thinking; without language there seems to be nothing like explicit thought whatever. All races of men—even the scattered, primitive denizens of the deep jungle, and brutish cannibals who have lived for centuries on world-removed islands—have their own complete and articulate language. There seems to be no simple, amorphous, or imperfect languages, such as one would naturally expect to find in conjunction with the lowest cultures. People who have not invented textiles, who live under roofs of pleated branches, need no privacy and mind to filth and roast their enemies for dinner, will yet converse over their bestial feasts in a tongue as grammatical as Greek, and as fluent as French. (p. 94)

What allows this transformation of idea to language to occur? What is the process of the transmission of the thought from one person to another? What ideational representations do we place out there in print and in the vapor of the space between people and institutions that lead to action or inaction, to political, social, and economic predispositions that permeate the common agreements that we have about how we understand and misunderstand each other and the institutions that we create to enforce and perpetuate them?

To begin a serious discussion of the language of the curriculum as it impacts on educational policy and practice I found myself looking closely at the form and function of language and how it is transmitted as a biological entity and a biological function. Karl Popper (cited in Blakemore, 1999) posited three worlds: (1) the physical world, (2) the world of subjective experiences (feelings, emotions, consciousness), and (3) the world of ideas (language, stories, art, technology, math, and science). The world of ideas and language has a life of its own and memetics provides a mechanism for its evolution.

Richard Dawkins (1989; cited in Blakemore, 1999) coined the term memes to represent those elements of culture that are passed on by imitation. These memes are selected from other memes in a pool, some of which are favored in a particular environment, and they cooperate in mutually supported memeplexes and are hostile to competing ones. The replication ability of the memes is the real unit of cultural transmission and evolution. Language is an example of this cultural evolution, as are fashion, dress, ceremonies, music, and catchphrases such as "excellence," "standards," "assessment," and "accountability" in education. As Dawkins noted (1989, pp. 192–193), the soup of culture is fueled by the replicator unit of memes as they leap from brain to brain by imitation. They take on the qualities of living structures that propagate in the mind and survive as an idea as they penetrate the cultural environment and exhibit a psychological appeal of common understandings. So these catchphrases are transmitted and understood through the propagation of memes by imitation of the idea of them. As a reflection of the subjectivity of consciousness, memes possess the ability to imitate, act selfishly for themselves, and exist in order to replicate. They act in their own self-interest and can produce behaviors that are mimetically adaptive. By "naming" things and ideas, we give them a boost in their quest for imitation and replication, building more and more memes around them that are maintained and grow in size and complexity. Once a name is given, it becomes a meme to contend with—it objectifies an idea or concept; for example, standardized testing takes on new meaning within and without the original context that it was designed to represent.

Blakemore (1999) states that memes jump from brain to brain, are stored in people's mind, in books, in language, and are passed on from person to person through imitation and objectified as "learning." Memes are not just objects; they can be representations of emotion, memory, and can spread around indiscriminately without regard to whether they are provoking, harmful, or neutral (p. 6). The meme cares not what effects it has, but only whether it is successful in doing what memes do, which is copy and spread. The scary part is that when they are ideas, they may spread regardless of their consequences; as they become more prolific, they may become false conceptualizations and we adopt all kinds of practices of belief around them.

Because memes are second replicators unique to human beings (genes also replicate what we pass on but they are primary replicators), they exhibit variation, such as the old game of "pass it on" where someone at the beginning of a line whispers something to the next person who passes it on to his or her next person and so on, until the end person who repeats what he/she hears articulates something entirely different from what the originator whispered. While something of the original is retained by copying it by example, the copy is not exact. New memes arising from the creativity of the mind come from this variation or combination of old ones in a person's mind, or from person to person. They are the tools that color how we think, and the mind is the replicating machinery and selective environment for the memes, the instructions for carrying out behavior. We think, act, and learn through imitation and instruction as we evolve personal ideas that are in the interest of the replicating memes (Blakemore, 1999).

While the spread of memes appears to be advantageous, in reality memes do not operate in that way. Memes compete (there is variety in theories of curriculum and instructional methodology, theories of learning, etc.) because they change the selective environment to the detriment of their competition—they shore up the environment that allows them to survive by increasing in complexity, design, without a goal in mind or an end point, except to become more complex and keep others at bay. So competition among ideas is not allowed in this process because the stronger and more complex meme always wins. It exhibits the best argument for sustainability and survival (p. 27). Examples in education include but are not limited to handwriting in the age of computers, rote memorization in the age of the Internet searches, or the basic structure of the educational organization that becomes more and more complex over time barring any other organizational structure.

The meme passes on information by language, reading material, and instruction. Learning is an adaptive mechanism that extends time and space by means of language and releasing memories by writing (Hall, 1969, 1973). This copying of ideas and behaviors from one person to another is possible because humans are consummate imitators and memes represent the smallest element that can replicate itself with fidelity, fecundity, and longevity, the three characteristics of a good replicator. Thus the replicator has to be copied accurately, many copies need to be made that are acceptable to the population, and the copies must last a long time or be referred to in the future (Dawkins, 1989). A good example in education is the progression of the standards movement from *A Nation at Risk* to the *No Child Left Behind* legislation. The solutions to the problems in education raised by each had fidelity as they were copied from site to site, fecundity across the country as classrooms began to look more and more alike in their approach to tested objectives, and longevity—it has been over twenty years since the first meme of accountability made its postmodern appearance. In addition, there are many areas where modern memes spread today because we have created vehicles for their ideological dissemination: schools, radio, television, newspapers, books, magazines, friends, and e-mail blogs, all of which are meme-spreading machines, and they attract consensus from the public because as memes they sustain themselves and thwart competition.

So, language and thought are by-products of our brains' ability to select which aspects of the world to imitate (Blakemore, 1999, p. 81). We talk and communicate, according to Dawkins (1989), to spread memes. While human language is innate (Pinker, 2000), human language capacity is meme driven and the function of language is to spread memes (Chomsky, 1998), to spread ideas. Language allowed our ancestors to acquire and pass on memes as information, to keep social groups together, to use symbols to stand for something else, to create ideas and to form a social contract for living within a society, and language is the prime mover for all this (Blakemore, 1999, p. 95). Langer (1951) believes that all genuine thinking is symbolic, and limits of expression are limits of conceptual power. But, language is more than symbols, she asserts; it is an organic functioning system whose parts are symbols. These parts integrate to make complex patterns that point to equally complex relationships in the world, the realm of meaning (p. 120). The sayings that the symbol is not the thing, the word is not the thing, the map is not the territory are apt here to underline the fact that the representation of memes is never fully true, as if we can ever know what is true or false.

Dawkins (1989) says there are selfish memes of indoctrination, and while humans are "built as gene machines, we are cultured as meme machines with the power to turn against our creators and rebel against the tyranny of the selfish replicators" (p. 201). So, there is room for change and for the creation of more useful memes. Thus, the biological function of language can be understood to be one of behavioral control, the transmission of information, the creation and expression of social cohesion, and/or the release of imagination and creativity.

Regarding the question of freedom from language, the following questions are posed:

1. How do ideas in education replicate? Can we trace the meme and chart its evolution, and can we explain the widespread use of certain memes that exclude thoughtful, more appropriate resolutions that have no opportunity to be spread and put into practice?
2. What is the survival value of an idea in education? Are some ideas able to survive at the expense of others, such as whole language versus phonics, because the meme for phonics is more easily imitated and spread? How can less spreadable memes be sustained and compete concerning decisions about curriculum and instruction? What conditions would create environments for alternative memes to penetrate the discussion about education?

3. What is the psychological appeal to our brains of ideas in education being tried over and over with little success but yet being applied in diverse venues (gendered schools; year round school; experiential learning, rote recitation, etc.)?

Language as Cultural/Social Control

> The creative achievements of human culture are the products of mimetic evolution, just as creative achievements of the biological world are the products of genetic evolution.
> (BLAKEMORE, 1999, P. 240).

> Pinker (2000) adds to this by saying, "The race is not to the swift but to the verbal" (p. 3).

The functionalist use of language as cultural/social control is that language use is for transmission of information to establish relationships among people. In addition, language provides a means of mutual expression, a vehicle to gain community and universal understanding, clarity of expression, and a vehicle to communicate with oneself. Chomsky (1998) says there is no proof that this is so. The Sapir Whorf hypothesis of linguistic development, which states that there is linguistic relativity that causes differences in thought of speakers of different languages, is also under attack by Pinker (2000) who asserts that thought is not the same as language, and that the legacy of Boas, Mead, Whorf, and Sapir is in error (p. 46). The idea that linguistic influence can control structure is being revised to that of cultural conventions and individual styles of people within a community. Meaning arises not in the text (written or spoken) but in the interpretation, and interpretation is shaped by context. Conventions, appropriate use, and the context of understanding are social understandings. In subcultures, the dominant conventions frame the phenomena; then we have the media perspective of transmission; then there is the individual's selective view of the world that tends to support or restrict certain kinds of observations and interpretations (Chandler, 2005). Chandler cites McLuhan's argument that the media is the cause of fundamental changes in society and in the human mind. Whether this is true or not, differences in language lead to differences in identification, and school represents a particular view of language in the learning of rules and prescriptions that culture accepts as correct, the scientific descriptive memes of truth. Ayers (1990, p. 28) wrote, "The difference between the man who used language scientifically and the man who used it emotively is not that the one produces sentences which are incapable of arousing emotion, and the other sentences which have no sense, but that the one is primarily concerned with the expression of true propositions, the other with the creation of a work of art."

Hayakawa and Hayakawa (1990) describe the language of everyday life as multivalued—that we see things in many ways and form value judgments of good, better, and best in both social and cultural situations. The multivalued orientation is better, they say, than a two-sided perspective since the latter makes for a competitive society that mobilizes to win, show up the other, rather than creating a forum for dialogue. Even within our field, we joust using language for position, for status and power, include or exclude based on ideology, rather than pool for action. Who has the best ideas, who can garner support and monies for their position, who publishes and dominates a field, as the memes duplicate not only programs but the rhetoric of success? Hayakawa and Hayakawa (1990, p. 68) warn that language is a means of social control; it objectifies social conventions, rules of the road, commerce, licenses, networks of agreement, all the details of the world that the words are supposed to bring about. With these agreements we have agreements about cooperation, peace, freedom, and social conformity of citizens to social and civic customs. Language is imbued with the lawyerese of our societal conventions along with the sanctions that go with them.

Chomsky (1998, p. 80) cites Foucault who described language as a by-product of bourgeoisie society. The task of the reformer is to gain power, not bring about more just society. The abstract justice one engages in is a class struggle to win, not because it leads to a more just society. You can win the war and lose the battle. The questions related to social and cultural control through language memes are just this: Are we losing the battle; has anything changed? Is there less poverty? Is there less homelessness? Are literacy rates going up? Are there more kids staying in school, leading to less unemployment and living standards below the poverty line? Do we etch in children's minds false maps that do not prepare them for life? What about the words we use to define the mission of education: excellence, quality, equity, fairness, and opportunity?

Language as Political Policy and Practice

In a *New York Times* article, Bumiller and Kornblut (September 18, 2005, p. 15) commented on the language used by President Bush post–hurricane Katrina concerning the issues of race and poverty. The power of meme-speak (my blatant takeoff on Orwell's Newspeak of *1984*, or the need for a Babel fish in *Hitchhiker's Guide to the Galaxy*) was in evidence with a shift from "compassionate conservative talk" that depicts the problem of blacks as largely economic to confrontational language of the civil rights era talking about "the legacy of inequality" while pledging billions of dollars to poor urban New Orleans. Bush's language echoed with new words citing images of "great divide" and of "race and class" in America. In the same article, the authors cite Barbara Bush who declared that many people in the relocation sites were faring better than they were before the storm since "so many of the people in the arena . . . were underprivileged anyway, so this is working very well for them."

Chomsky (1998) wrote that the language of racism is grounded in historical empiricism and in a blank slate account of learning that is manipulative. The rationalist model is concerned with the active creative mind neither imposed on from without nor from within, but upholding the dignity of the person. Freedom, rather than a meme of imitation, should be, Chomsky says, a self-activity of thinking with reform being the battle against the barriers of social change that defend established privilege (pp. 129–131).

Language use when creating policy and practice is powerful. Just look at the recent senate hearings for John Roberts. Editorials abound in the press analyzing one word, one meme, that of "privacy"—what did the founders mean by it, does it extend to personal choice, and how did it become a meme metaphor for abortion rights and the overturning of *Roe v. Wade?* Memes are used as tools to make judgments and conclusions about right and wrong, good and evil, humanity and exploitation. The most powerful meme is democracy, yet we war and conquer, taking note of mutivalued orientations based on our own prejudices of the term, of the meme that, we believe, should be imitated. The foundation of our society is memes. These statements of agreement concerning future events aim to predict behavior based on common imitation and practice. There are true opportunities for peace and freedom, we believe, based on the imposition of behavioral imitation supported by powerful words and symbols (i.e., the eagle, the flag, the capital buildings, rites and rituals of government). The collective sanctions of our constitution, laws, oaths, praise and punishments, feasts to commemorate our heritage, and their repetition over time cement the memes of use as they grow larger than life and become less flexible and adaptable to the temper of the time.

In *Language in Thought and Action* Hayakawa and Hayakawa (1990) wrote that the role of language in biological and functional life is to persuade, control behavior, transmit information, create and express social cohesion, and allow for poetry and imagination (p. x). The communicative function uses mass media, the press, movies, television, and the Internet to help raise aspirations of people as they strive to be like others and this is facilitated by imitating memes. The world keeps going on the collected wisdom, information that helps control the environment from one generation to the next, creating cultural and intellectual cooperation that we take for granted in our meme-driven world. Hayakawa and Hayakawa say people are immersed in words, they live in their heads, in a "Niagara of words" (p. 10), and ideas are "cerebral itches that are verbalized" (p. 11) in the semantic environment. Survival of the fittest requires the ability to talk, write, listen, read, and understand—the power of which is described by Freire (1970). Little of the symbolic nature of the verbal world is experienced firsthand, so we get our information, or imitated memes, from other sources, and we live in two worlds, the world of what is going on around us and the verbal world we do not experience firsthand. S. I. Hayakawa and A. R. Hayakawa called this the "map of the territory" and, if it is a true map, you are prepared for life; if it is a false map, then you are not prepared because the imitator believes the prejudices of maps that are presented are the territory. Hayakawa says teachers cannot help passing on certain misinformation and error (p. 103). How then can we provide better, truer maps of the territory for teaching and learning? How can we teach so we discard the useless knowledge, the errors of information? The false maps are those of prejudice, bias, despair, all that have to be replaced by hope, participation, and the seeking of truth. We believe that the map, the meme, is scientifically based, and if its source is those we have elected to positions of authority or those who have positions of wealth and/or power, then they are true maps of experience. This is not so.

Some in our field place blame and look for signs of false maps and memes that limit individual freedom and equality; others rely on experimentation and science as true evidence of verifiable maps; still others listen to judgments from outside the field and seek approval for a job well done that is in line with the popular imposed regulations that limit pedagogical and theoretical theories. These positions deny inherent bias and false conclusions about occurrences, persons, or programs (i.e., here we go again with single-gendered schools, a recent front page innovation in *The Miami Herald*)—that sells memes directly to the public so they can look for evidence of imitation in their own schools. Maps pile up independent of the territory, and they are meaningless noises that bear no relation to reality, yet elicit automatic reactions; they are confusing jumbles of words used to describe words, oververbalizations that are circular and have the effect of freezing behavior (Hayakawa and Hayakawa 1990, p. 145).

The language of the curriculum is characterized by these oververbalizations, smoke screens for action and ideas, guided by words alone rather than facts that should guide us. But, Hayakawa and Hayakawa (1990) say, when the rich and powerful, the wielders of policy, are shortsighted or irresponsible, they need help from those who are not powerful to be able to hold back institutional adjustments. We, curriculum workers, should not aid and abet the false maps, the memes of practice, which have taken over the language of the field. Two-dimensional woman or man is incapable of changing behavior, but we seem to be using the same dysfunctional behavior over and over, until a nervous breakdown happens, like a rat which, trying the same solution over and over again, becomes sick of trying or gets confused when there are too many choices. We cannot be disillusioned with the process of using the language of the field. We have to create and imitate memes that lead to more appropriate ends.

Concluding Meme

In 1838, Horace Mann (cited in Cremin, 1957) wrote about language in his Second Annual Report. Mann offers a compelling possibility that without language, we can only know the immediate that we personally experience, and an impenetrable wall of darkness would lie beyond "[a] narrow horizon . . . With language, that horizon recedes until the expanse of the globe, with its continents, its air, its oceans, and all that are therein, lies under our eye . . . antiquity re-lives; . . . the long train of historic events passes in review before us; . . . we behold the multiplication of our race, from individuals to nations, from patriarchs to dynasties; . . . the rise and fall of empires; we see the dealings of God with men, and of men with each other;—all, in fine, which has been done and suffered by our kindred nature, in arms, arts, science, philosophy, judicature, government; and we see them, not by their own light only, but by the clearer light reflected upon them from subsequent times" (p. 36).

The memes of language can do all this and more. But, we have to be open and aware of misinterpretations and of the meme that changes practice, pushing out big memes of ideas that should be kept as part of our educational heritage and mission. In July 2005, in his remarks at the AFT QuEST conference, Jack Jennings (*American Educator*, 2005, pp. 4–5), president of the Center on Education Policy, and a pioneer of the 1960s ESEA, asserted that the successor to the ESEA legislation is the No Child Left Behind Act (NCLB). He stated that the 1960s equity goals of civil rights remain at its core by requiring that all children be proficient by 2014. The law holds schools accountable for education for all, especially targeted at every race, ethnic group, the poor, English limited, and children with disabilities. In addition, it requires there be highly qualified teachers to help those most in need of this equity goal in order to close the achievement gap. Controversial remedies that have spread as memes to achieve this goal, Jennings asserts, are the timelines, penalties and funding, and more importantly the question whether the legislation is an intrusion on state and local control of education. Of course there are other concerns: how to create good assessment for accountability; what is needed to turn around poor performing schools, including monies needed and their source, to fund programs and services; what is meant by highly qualified teachers and how can experienced teachers be coaxed into the lowest performing schools? At the end of his remarks Jennings called for critics to show how the goals of the legislation can be attained by improvement in schools. He called for educators to not be penalized, but rather be engaged in the dialogue and fight for their ideas, but fight effectively, to get their ideas in place. Rather than letting the memes of imitation of programs and ideas control the endless duplication, let those on the front lines, who know the student population best, work toward the goals of equity instead of having the solutions come to them ready made and impenetrable.

The language we curriculum workers use is often dichotomized into good and bad, right and wrong, as the words become accepted as having value dimensions that are backed by scientific proof and self-fulfilling expectations. The big issues of democracy, success, cooperation, humanity, equity, and equality—all these require another form of thought and language that is open and inclusive, multifaceted and multivalued in society. These require orientations that are open to debate and dialogue so that they truly reflect the underlying values of a society and provide for orientations that are focused on societal advancement. Curriculum workers are charged with advising and consenting on matters of policy and practice, so we have to be careful what memes we aid and abet and which ones we as yet have the opportunity to create.

References

Adams, D. (1995). *Hitchhiker's Guide to the Galaxy*. New York: Ballantine Books.
Ayers, A. J. (1990). *Language, Truth and Logic*. New York: Penguin Books.
Blakemore, S. (1999). *The Meme Machine*. Oxford: Oxford University.
Bumiller, E., and Kornblut, A. E. (2005). Black Leaders Say Storm Forced Bush to Confront Issues of Race and Poverty. *New York Times*, September 18, p. 15.
Chandler, D. (2005). *The Sapir-Whorf Hypothesis*. http://www.aber.ac.uk/media/Documents/short/whorf.html, accessed September 8, 2005.
Chomsky, N. (1998). *On Language*. New York: New Press.
Cremin, L. (Ed.) (1957). *The Republic and the School: Horace Mann on the Education of Free Men*. New York: Teachers College Press.
Dawkins, R. (1989). *The Selfish Gene*. Oxford: Oxford University.
Freire, P. (1970). *Pedagogy of the Oppressed*. New York: Seabury Press.
Hall, E. T. (1969). *The Hidden Dimension*. New York: Doubleday.
———. (1973). *The Silent Language*. New York: Doubleday.
Hayakawa, S. I., and Hayakawa, A. R. (1990). *Language in Thought and Action*. San Diego: Harcourt.
Jennings, J. (2005). The Federal Role in Education: Looking Back, Moving Forward. *American Educator* (Fall), pp. 4–5.
Langer, S. K. (1951). *Philosophy in a New Key*. New York: Mentor Books.
Mann, H. (1957). Edited by L.A. Cremin. *The Republic and the School: Horace Mann on the Education of Free Man*. New York: Teachers College Press.
Orwell, G. (1961). *1984*. New York: New American Library.
Pinker, S. (2000). *The Language Instinct*. New York: Harper Collins.

Epilogue

The Evolution of the American Creed

Survival of the Fittest

STEPHEN M. FAIN, DAVID M. CALLEJO PEREZ, JUDITH J. SLATER

In 1835 Alexis de Tocqueville offered the following observation, "People in America obey the law, not only because it is their work, but because it may be changed, if it be harmful; a law is observed because, first, it is a self-imposed evil, and secondly, it is an evil of transient duration" (Heffner, 1956, pp. 107–108). This observation may be considered, at least in part, as conformation of the commitment made by the founders to principles they saw as fundamental in building a nation consisting of "life, liberty, and the pursuit of happiness (The Declaration of Independence, 1776 www.ushistory.org/declaration/document/index.htm). The struggle for a more perfect union (The Constitution of the United States of America, 1787, www.ushistory.org/documents/constitution.htm), and the basic protections assured all citizens (Bill of Rights, 1789, www.ushistory.org/documents/amendments.htm) remain as the bedrock of our democracy.

Anatol Lieven (2004) explains that Ralph Waldo Emerson described "the adherence to American governing principles as a form of religious conversion" (p. 48), and historian Richard Hofstadter wrote, "it has been our fate as a nation not to have ideologies but to be one" (p. 49). Lieven examines what he calls the American Creed, whose essential elements "are faith in liberty, constitutionalism, the law, democracy, individualism and cultural and political egalitarianism" (p. 49). This idea of an American Creed resonates with most citizens today. Many recall Superman as a champion of the values outlined above; even though as Robert Bellah noted principles central to the creed today often go unexamined by the citizenry.

It appears that the spirit of this American Creed is a constant; more accepted than examined; used by leaders as a platform to shape and reshape our "America," and serves as a benchmark for the history of our nation. For example, in his "House Divided" speech in 1858, Abraham Lincoln clearly reminded Americans of the centrality of the Union. He said:

> A house divided against itself cannot stand. I believe this government cannot endure permanently half slave and half free. I do not expect the Union to be dissolved—I do not expect the house to fall—but I do expect it will cease to be divided. It will become all one thing, or all the other.[1]

Seven years later, in his Second Inaugural address, President Lincoln returned to the theme of national unity. Lincoln spoke:

> With malice toward none, with charity for all, with firmness in the right as God gives us to see the right, let us strive on to finish the work we are in, to bind up the nation's wounds, to care for him who shall have borne the battle and for his widow and his orphan, to do all which may achieve and cherish a just and lasting peace among ourselves and with all nations.[2]

The healing process was slow but it created a national identity of one nation. That may have a great deal to do with the way Lincoln stressed the tie binding the American citizen to the Union as pointed out by Samuel Elito Morison (1965) who noted that "He [Lincoln] made the average American feel that his dignity as a citizen of the republic was bound up with the fate of the Union, whose destruction would be a victory for enemies of freedom everywhere" (p. 618).

As we evolved so did our laws and social policies, revealing that the faith put into our constitution is justified. In the aftermath of the Civil War the growth of the United States was remarkable. The growth of American industry and the fortunes amassed by the industrialist were unheard of, the streaming in of immigrants was literally overwhelming in many American cities and centers of industry. A new political structure began to evolve as new citizens clustered in ethnic enclaves and formed new ethnically centered local political machines that controlled politics through the typical boss—its blend of charity and patronage. These political machines were built on a public that had become citizens and had heard the words life, liberty, and the pursuit of happiness but most likely had no idea what these words meant (Handlin, 1951, pp. 201–226). Additionally, labor gained a voice as the union movement grew along with American industry. The frontier days of the nation were clearly behind and a new nation was evolving.

Theodore Roosevelt responded to the conditions facing America when on September 7, 1903, he called for a "Square Deal" for all Americans:

> We must act upon the motto of all for each and each for all. There must be ever present in our minds the fundamental truth that in a republic such as ours the only safety is to stand neither for nor against any man because he is rich or because he is poor, because he is engaged in one occupation or another, because he works with his brains or because he works with his hands. We must treat each man on his worth and merits as a man. We must see that each is given a square deal, because he is entitled to no more and should receive no less. Finally, we must keep ever in mind that a republic such as ours can exist only by virtue of the orderly liberty which comes through the equal domination of the law over all men alike, and through its administration in such resolute and fearless fashion as shall teach all that no man is above it and no man below it.[3]

Roosevelt, along with Presidents Taft and Wilson, was influenced by the Progressive Movement that swept the United States at the turn of the twentieth century. In 1913, Wilson referred to the social contract between the nation and its people as "New Freedom." This was a declaration of separation from the past styles of operation of government while asserting the centrality of the basic principles of life, liberty, and the pursuit of happiness. Wilson observed that "some citizens of this country have never got beyond the Declaration of Independence, signed in Philadelphia, July 4th, 1776. Their bosoms swell against George III, but they have no consciousness of the war for freedom that is going on to-day."[4]

The issues of the day were complex. President Wilson explains the times as follows:

> What form does the contest between tyranny and freedom take to-day? What is the special form of tyranny we now fight? How does it endanger the rights of the people, and what do we mean to do in order to make our contest against it effectual? What are to be the items of our new declaration of independence?
>
> By tyranny, as we now fight it, we mean control of the law, of legislation and adjudication, by organizations which do not represent the people, by means which are private and selfish. We mean, specifically, the conduct of our affairs and the shaping of our legislation in the interest of special bodies of capital and those who organize their use. We mean the alliance, for this purpose, of political machines with selfish business. We mean the exploitation of the people by legal and political means. We have seen many of our governments under these influences cease to be representative governments, cease to be governments representative of the people, and become governments representative of special interests, controlled by machines, which in their turn are not controlled by the people.[5]

Theodore Roosevelt's "Square Deal" and Woodrow Wilson's "New Freedom" were intended to resonate with the people. In just a few words the spirit of the concept was so effectively captured that there was really no reason for the common citizen to examine the program. The concept of a "Square Deal" called out for fairness for all; the concept of "New Freedom" was constructed by making a connection to independence and the principles of life, liberty and the pursuit of happiness in a new America; and Franklin Delano Roosevelt's "New Deal" promised to Americans approximately three decades of adjustments in the application of fundamental American principles to a national landscape that was radically different from that of 1776. The language used when casting these phrases was rich in allusion to the American creed and it resonated with citizens who may have never reflected on the deeper meanings of the U.S. Constitution and the Bill or Rights but who valued the American Creed. The spirit of the Creed in 1941 was captured by FDR in his Four Freedoms Speech (1941).

The American people embraced the American Creed even more strongly after World War II, as the nation defeated tyrants and defended freedom and democracy. The principles for which the nation had fought were more celebrated than examined by most Americans. The victory of democracy over fascism strengthened the people's resolve to sustain their democracy.

President Truman began the integration of the U.S. military in 1946, appointing the President's Committee on Civil Rights. For the first time, the United States made a concerted effort to reintegrate its military into society by passing the GI Bill that provided low-cost loans, job and college training, and medical care for all veterans of the military. President Dwight Eisenhower continued Truman's commitment to reduce racial discrimination that was glaring in the South and persistent across the nation. Additionally, President Eisenhower approved an increase in Social Security, opened the borders of the United States by leading in the passage of the Refugee Relief Act of 1953; in 1957 he federalized National Guardsman and directed them to control the people and protect the African American students who were to integrate Little Rock High School. The man who toured the concentration camps of Germany at the end of World War II declared, "There must be no second class citizens in this country."[6] These efforts were consistent with the American Creed, and by advancing Civil Rights Americans tested themselves as many had to come face to face with their race prejudice and fear.

In the post–World War II years, the enemy was clearly identified as Communism. For instance, in schools across the nations courses were introduced pitting Democracy against Communism and directing the students to consider the basic differences between the ideologies by comparing the U.S. Constitution (including the Bill of Rights) with the Communist Manifesto (1848). However, Americans understood that it was more than economic systems that separated them from the citizens of the Soviet Union. In the USSR there was no freedom of speech, freedom of religion, freedom from want, freedom from fear. Keenly aware of the growing fear of Communism and the potential for a major shift on the American landscape, President Eisenhower spoke to the people of America as he left the presidency in 1961:

Until the latest of our world conflicts, the United States had no armaments industry. American makers of plowshares could, with time and as required, make swords as well. But now we can no longer risk emergency improvisation of national defense; we have been compelled to create a permanent armaments industry of vast proportions. Added to this, three and a half million men and women are directly engaged in the defense establishment. We annually spend on military security more than the net income of all United States corporations.

This conjunction of an immense military establishment and a large arms industry is new in the American experience. The total influence—economic, political, even spiritual—is felt in every city, every Statehouse, every office of the Federal government. We recognize the imperative need for this development. Yet we must not fail to comprehend its grave implications. Our toil, resources and livelihood are all involved; so is the very structure of our society.

In the councils of government, we must guard against the acquisition of unwarranted influence, whether sought or unsought, by the military-industrial complex. The potential for the disastrous rise of misplaced power exists and will persist.[7]

Sixty years separate FDR's Four Freedoms Speech and the terrorist attack on the World Trade Center on September 11, 2001. There is little evidence to suggest that the people of America had a better understanding of the U.S. Constitution and the Bill of Rights in 2001 than those who first heard Roosevelt's speech. Eleven men have served as President between FDR and September 11, 2001. And in varying degrees they have maintained the trust of the American people by adhering to the American Creed. Their commitment to the principles of faith in liberty, constitutionalism, the law, democracy, individualism and cultural and political egalitarianism has been their connection to the citizenry they governed. Approximately fifty years stand between Eisenhower's refinement of social programs intended to provide opportunity and support and his warning to the citizens to be watchful of the military-industrial complex. Forty years have passed since Lyndon Johnson declared a "War on Poverty" and proclaimed that America could be a "Great Society" where poverty and racial injustice would be replaced with abundance and liberty for all.

Approximately twenty years before the terrorists struck on 9/11, President Ronald Reagan put forth the proposition of a "New Federalism." He challenged Americans to look to the federal government for less. He said: "It is my intention to curb the size and influence of the Federal establishment and to demand recognition of the distinction between the powers granted to the federal government and those reserved to the states or to the people" (Presidential Inaugural Address, 1981). Appealing to the strong association Americans have with the American Creed, this shift in the locus of control was consistent with their unexamined belief in the principles of faith in liberty, constitutionalism, the law, democracy, individualism, and cultural and political egalitarianism of liberty and independence. The "New Federalism" was embraced by Americans. Not only did it make good cultural sense, it also was consistent with the basic freedoms Americans had come to associate with life in their country. The new approach from the nation's capitol was linked directly to the freedoms Americans understood was their birthright. Presidential administrations have taken the lead in reshaping the supportive liberal conception of welfare to a more conservative or traditional view of welfare as weakness and independence as self-sufficiency as strength. For many staunch liberal democrats focused on issues within the country, Reagan attracted with a strong voice calling for the nation to protect itself and other nations from the possibility of nuclear attack from the "evil empire" (the Soviet Union).[8] Seeking freedom from fear these neoconservatives now aligned with Republicans believing that the strongest defense lay in the maintaining the strongest offense.

On the morning of September 11, 2001, nineteen terrorists, all affiliated with al-Qaeda, highjacked four commercial airlines and changed world history when two flew into the World Trade Center Towers in New York City and one struck the Pentagon. President George W. Bush addressed the nation:

> Today, our fellow citizens, our way of life, our very freedom came under attack in a series of deliberate and deadly terrorist acts. The victims were in airplanes, or in their offices; secretaries, businessmen and women, military and federal workers; moms and dads, friends and neighbors. Thousands of lives were suddenly ended by evil, despicable acts of terror.
>
> A great people has been moved to defend a great nation. Terrorist attacks can shake the foundations of our biggest buildings, but they cannot touch the foundation of America. These acts shattered steel, but they cannot dent the steel of American resolve.
>
> America was targeted for attack because we're the brightest beacon for freedom and opportunity in the world. And no one will keep that light from shining...
>
> This is a day when all Americans from every walk of life unite in our resolve for justice and peace. America has stood down enemies before, and we will do so this time. None of us will ever forget this day. Yet, we go forward to defend freedom and all that is good and just in our world.[9]

Just nine days later before a joint session of Congress the President declared war on terror:

> We have seen the state of our Union in the endurance of rescuers, working past exhaustion. We have seen the unfurling of flags, the lighting of candles, the giving of blood,

the saying of prayers—in English, Hebrew, and Arabic. We have seen the decency of a loving and giving people who have made the grief of strangers their own.

My fellow citizens, for the last nine days, the entire world has seen for itself the state of our Union—and it is strong.

Tonight we are a country awakened to danger and called to defend freedom. Our grief has turned to anger, and anger to resolution. Whether we bring our enemies to justice, or bring justice to our enemies, justice will be done.

Our war on terror begins with al Qaeda, but it does not end there. It will not end until every terrorist group of global reach has been found, stopped and defeated.[10]

The strong words of the President echoed across America—they were consistent with the American Creed. Americans believed that their way of life was indeed threatened.

The American Nation: Notions of Democracy Today

In the chapters within this book, the authors have attempted to use political, social, economic, and personal narratives to explain the nature of American identity. It is our argument that we rarely examine those basic notions that make our identity unique. It becomes an act of futility to question who we are in terms of what we believe. If this is case, we risk losing the feel and practice of the moral tradition of the U.S. Constitution expressed in Franklin Roosevelt's Four Freedoms.

Gripped by fear and bound to our notions of nationhood, we have allowed ourselves to further de-emphasize what our rights and freedoms are under our laws. In "Power of the Powerless," Vaclav Havel (1986a) ponders about the state of mind of a fruit and vegetable store manager in a totalitarian state who places a sign with a slogan that reads "Workers of the World Unite!" on his storefront window. Havel asks: why does he do it? Is he making a statement about unity of all workers? Does he understand its meaning? Or has it been lost in years of ritualism? (p. 41). What the store owner understands is that by not placing the sign on his window he communicates his desire to question the state, and risks punishment. Further, I also assert that the store owner goes about his everyday business without thinking about his condition, feeling as one with his fellow citizens, institutions, and the world. He has a moral and spiritual connection to his enterprise. However, his consolidated view of society is far from the actual reality. For example, in the global economy, poverty grows, intolerance increases, and wars linger for years. So how do we spiral deeper into this schism without reflection; why, as Havel asks, "are people in fact behaving in the way they do?" He concludes that "for any unprejudiced observer, the answer is . . . self-evident: they are driven by fear" (Havel, 1986b, p. 4).

It is almost trite to suggest that fundamental to the character of the American people is their unexamined but deeply held belief that all Americans are entitled to basic rights that ensure liberty and freedom (Bellah et al., 1985). In our era that means security at all costs, including those like freedom and liberty, personal rights, and simple generalizations that allow us to further bury the meanings of life, liberty, and pursuit of happiness. In *Summer Meditations,* Havel (1992) writes, "I feel that the dormant goodwill in people needs to be stirred. People need to hear that it makes sense to behave decently or to help others."[11] In the state of our country, we need to ask what is occurring when it is Bill Maher in an HBO show held on Friday nights who is speaking of the spirit of the U.S. Constitution and who is critically examining the Bill of Rights, when it is the media, public intellectuals, and universities who should be doing it.

American national identity is at an important crossroads in 2006. The disagreements among the federal government and its people as to what government should do have disappeared. In 2001 most Americans and their political leaders concurred that the future of the United States should be based on a security and economic model that seeks a successful insertion for the United States as a "City Upon a Hill" in particular, and in the world as the eternal soldier against terrorism.

The United States' dominance of economic, political, and military development within the world (especially within the UN) has also broadened its political control of the federal state over the political and social affairs of its people, by virtue of the centralization of decision making that what is good for America is good for the world.

The implication of this is that the American fight against terrorism faces a crucial moment. It must redefine its nationalist identity first, and then its relation to its people and the world. Moreover, the elections of 2004 gave George W. Bush's Republican Party (GOP) absolute majority in the Congress. The GOP has emphasized centralization and the reduction of the privileges of the minorities (racial, economic, sexual, etc.) while emphasizing the benefits of the economic elite. For the first time, the outcome of the elections has given the federal government a green light to draft and implement its own "American" policies, without the need to seek congressional support by others. The electoral success of the GOP was based mainly on the state of fear (Terrorism) of the American people and nation, not on its handling of other issues, such as economic development, protection of civil rights or economic welfare. The result of the elections resulted in a partisan partnership linking the Executive and the Legislative branches of government ideologically. The power of this relationship provided an opportunity for bringing the Judicial branch into line with the others. Clearly, when the checks and balances of government are closely aligned, the natural tendency of agreement takes the place of the otherwise natural adversarial relationship that should produce rigorous debate and enlightened decision-making.

Although there may be disagreement about politics, we believe that the Four Freedoms articulated by FDR provide a standard for assessing the state of democracy within the United States and everywhere in the world. As we consider the priorities nations are establishing for educational standards across the oceans of the world, we are struck with the neglect of programs designed to create world citizens who value FDR's Four Freedoms as fundamental to democratic life in the twenty-first century.

Notes

1. http://www.historyplace.com/lincoln/divided.htm. Retrieved October 3, 2006.
2. http://www.bartleby.com/124/pres32.html. Retrieved October 3, 2006.
3. http://www.theodore-roosevelt.com/trsquaredealspeech.html. Retrieved October 3, 2006.
4. http://www.vindicatingthefounders.com/library/index.asp?document=48. Retrieved October 3, 2006.
5. Ibid. http://www.vindicatingthefounders.com/library/index.asp?document=48. Retrieved October 3, 2006.
6. Quoted in Morison, 1956, p. 1087
7. Eisenhower's Farewell Address to the Nation, January 17, 1961. http://mcadams.posc.mu.edu/ike.htm. Retrieved October 3, 2006.
8. See Howard Zinn, 2005, pp. 578–600.
9. Statement by the President in His Address to the Nation, September 11, 2001. http://www.whitehouse.gov/news/releases/2001/09/20010911–16.html. Retrieved October 3, 2006.
10. Address to a Joint Session of Congress and the American People, September 20, 2001. http://www.whitehouse.gov/news/releases/2001/09/20010920-8.html. Retrieved October 3, 2006.
11. See (Havel, 1986b) pp. 1–21. This quote comes from p. 8, where Havel wonders what took so long for the Soviet control to be overturned and how unbridled capitalism has a tendency to emphasize oppression and inequality. In the end, he believes, it is the individual's quest for democracy that leads to change.

References

Bellah, R., R. Madsen, W. Sullivan, A. Swindler, and S. Tipton (1985). *Habits of Heart: Individualism and Commitment in American Life*. Berkeley, CA: University of California Press.

Bill of Rights (1789). www.ushistory.org/documents/amendments.htm. Retrieved October 5, 2006.

The Constitution of the United States of America (1787) www.ushistory.org/documents/constitution.htm. Retrieved October 5, 2006.

The Declaration of Independence (1776). www.ushistory.org/declaration/document/index.htm. Retrieved October 5, 2006.

Handlin, O. (1951). *The Uprooted: The Epic Story of the Great Migration that Made the American People.* New York: Grossett & Dunlap.

Heffner, R. D. (Ed.). (1956). *Alexis de Tocqueville: A Democracy in America.* New York: A Mentor Book; Penguin Books.

Havel, V. (1986a). Power of the Powerless. In J. Vladislav (Ed.), *Vaclav Havel or Living in Truth* (pp. 36–122). London: Farber and Farber.

———. (1986b) Letter to Gustav Husak. In J. Vladislav (Ed.), *Vaclav Havel or Living in Truth* (pp. 3–35). London: Farber and Farber.

———. (1992). *Summer Meditations.* New York: Alfred Knopf.

Lieven, A. (2004). *America Right or Wrong: An Anatomy of American Nationalism.* New York: Oxford University Press.

Morison, S. E. (1965). *History of the American People.* New York: Oxford University Press.

Reagan, R. (January 20, 1981). *Presidential Inaugural Address.* http://www.yale.edu/lawweb/avalon/presiden/inaug/reagan1.htm. Retrieved October 4, 2006.

Zinn, H. (2005). *A Peoples History of the United States: 1492–Present.* New York: Harper Perennial Modern Classics.

Contributors

Leon D. Caldwell, Ph.D. is currently a research associate professor in the psychology department at the University of Memphis while on leave as an Associate Professor of Educational Psychology at the University of Nebraska, Lincoln. He received his doctorate from Penn State in counseling psychology and a Master's in Secondary Counseling and Bachelor's in Economics. His research and publications include school based health promotion interventions, African American student health, and prevention intervention research.

David M. Callejo Pérez teaches curriculum studies and coordinates the doctoral program in Curriculum and Instruction at West Virginia University. He co-edited *Pedagogy of Place* (2004) and wrote *Southern Hospitality* (2001). His work focuses on identity and schools, teacher education, qualitative research, and transmigration.

After earning a B.A. in Russian at Duke University, **Jennifer Deets** served as a Military Intelligence officer in the U.S. Army. During Desert Storm in 1991, she served with the 1st Armored Division in Saudi Arabia, Iraq, and Kuwait. After leaving active service, she studied Slavic Linguistics and then Curriculum Studies, earning her Ph.D. at the University of Texas at Austin in 1998. During six years of teaching at the University of Central Florida, Jennifer pursued an extensive research project on homeschooling, including two years of homeschooling her own children. Her book, *Seasons of learning: Homeschooling in Ethnographic Perspective* is currently with her editor at Penn Press. She now teaches at the University of North Carolina at Wilmington and is active in the educational community as a volunteer and consultant. Her favorite flag is the one presented to her by her father; it had flown over the Capitol on the day of her commissioning.

Stephen M. Fain is Professor Emeritus at Florida International University where he is taught curriculum history and theory for the past 30 years. Additionally, he is a fellow in the Honors College, where he teaches a year-long course on discovering the American Character. His research interests include the evolution of the American System of Education. He holds an Ed.D. from Teachers College, Columbia University. Steve has also co-edited Pedagogy of Place (Peter Lang, 2004) and The Freiran Legacy (Peter Lang, 2002).

Arthur Frakt retired as the Dean of the Law School and Vice President of Widener University in Pennsylvania and Delaware. He had previously been Dean and Professor of Law at Loyola Law School of Los Angeles. He had spent sixteen years as a Professor and sometime Associate Dean at Rutgers Law School Camden. Frakt began his legal career as Deputy Attorney General for Civil Rights in New Jersey and served on the State Boards of the ACLU in New Jersey and Delaware and as the Chairman of the South Jersey Civil Liberties Union. He is currently the principal consultant to Drexel University for their newly founded College of Law

David J. R. Frakt is Associate Professor of Law and Director of the Criminal Law Practice Center at Western State University College of Law, Fullerton, Ca. Prof Frakt earned his B.A. in History summa cum laude, from the University of California, Irvine. He received his J.D., cum laude, from Harvard Law School. After law school, Professor Frakt served as a law clerk to the Honorable Monroe G. McKay, formerly Chief Judge of the United States Court of Appeals for the Tenth Circuit. After his clerkship, Professor Frakt was commissioned as a First Lieutenant in the United States Air Force Judge Advocate General's Corps. He served on active duty for nearly ten years, before becoming a professor and transitioning to the US Air Force Reserves. In 2003, Professor Frakt was awarded the Younger Federal Lawyer Award from the Federal Bar Association. Professor Frakt is a member of the New Jersey Bar.

Robert Gutierrez was a classroom teacher of twenty-five years (Pinellas, FL, and Miami-Dade, FL, school districts). His bachelor's and master's degrees were attained from Florida State University in 1970 and 1972 respectively. He received his educational doctorate from Florida International University in 1998. Since 2000, he has been assistant professor at Florida State University. There he is serving as coordinator of the social science education program. His research interests have been in area of civic education where he has several articles published including a study on the predispositions of high school students regarding civic problem solving.

Lesley A. Northup is Associate Professor of Religious Studies and Associate Dean of the Honors College at Florida International University. Dr. Northup's research focuses on American religion, especially in the areas of church and state, religion and sexuality, contemporary religious movements, ritual studies, and mythography. She has produced four edited or single-authored books, four volumes of the reference work *Religious Documents of North America Annual*, and numerous articles and reviews. She is the recipient of numerous teaching awards

Anne Marie Pagliaro is a Professor of Nursing at the University of Alberta, Canada. Her research interests seeks to answer the question of why people use drugs and substances of abuse, a question of concern to many, including nursing educators, practitioners, and researchers. Anne Marie has co-written or written over 15 books, numerous articles, and abstracts on numerous topics including nursing practice and addiction. She is currently the Director of the Substance Abusology Research Group.

Louis A. Pagliaro is a Professor in the Department of Educational Psychology at the University of Alberta. Dr. Pagliaro's other notable academic and professional accomplishments include: former Professor of Pharmacy and Pharmaceutical Sciences and former President of the College of Alberta Psychologists. He is a Fellow of the American Board of Medical Psychotherapists and a Fellow of the Prescribing Psychologists Register. Dr. Pagliaro has authored or co-authored several hundred publications since becoming a member of the academic staff at the University of Alberta in 1977, including 13 textbooks. His research interests include substance abuse education and treatment, the effects of drugs and substances of abuse on cognition, learning, memory, and behavior; and the psychology of youth gang behavior, bullying and terrorism

Steven Selden is Professor in the Curriculum Theory and Development program at the University of Maryland College Park. He received a Fulbright Lectureship at the Beijing Normal University in 1994, and is the recipient of the University of Maryland's College of Education's Vernon Anderson Outstanding Faculty Award. He serves as Scholarly Advisor to the United States Holocaust Museum program, "Deadly Medicine: Creating the Master Race, and the *Digital Archive of American Eugenics*. His publications include, *Inheriting Shame: The Story of Eugenics and*

Racism in America (1999), and "Who's Paying for the Culture Wars?" *Academe,* Sept-Oct 2005.

Judith J. Slater is Professor of Curriculum and Instruction, Florida International University, retired. Her book publications include Anatomy of a Collaboration, Acts of Alignment, The Freirean Legacy, Pedagogy of Place, and Teen Life in Asia.

Pablo Toral is a Mouat Junior Professor of International Studies at Beloit College, Beloit, Wisconsin. He has published articles about Spanish multinational enterprises and their activities in Latin America, regional integration in the Americas, and about nationalism, education and identity in Spain. He is the author of The Reconquest of the New World. Spain's Multinational Enterprises and Direct Investment in Latin America and Latin America's Quest for Globalization. The Role of Spanish Firms. He also serves as a consultant. Before becoming an academic, Toral worked as a journalist in Latin America, the United States, and Europe.

Donn C. Worgs, Ph. D. is currently an assistant professor of Political Science and Director of the Metropolitan Studies Program at Towson University. He received his doctorate from the University of Maryland, College Park. His current research focuses on civic engagement around education in urban communities and African American political behavior.